Callsign
GRAY EAGLE

LIFE STORIES FROM AN AIRCRAFT CARRIER SAILOR

For Dot

Callsign
GRAY EAGLE

LIFE STORIES FROM AN AIRCRAFT CARRIER SAILOR

Lynn B. Smith

Lynn B. Smith
Enterprise, Alabama

Lynn B. Smith
callsigngrayeagle@outlook.com

Book Layout ©2017 BookDesignTemplates.com

Callsign **GRAY EAGLE**, Life Stories from an Aircraft Carrier Sailor / Lynn B. Smith. —1st ed.
ISBN 978-1-7342157-0-0

To all who served in USS Ranger CVA/CV-61
and
To those who waited for their sailors to come home, they also served.

Do It Now

"I expect pass through this world but once.
Any good thing therefore that I can do
or any kindness that I can show to any fellow human being,
let me do it now.
Let me not defer nor neglect it;
for I shall not pass this way again."

—Stephan Grellet

Many years ago my children presented these words of wisdom to me on a plaque that hangs in my office still.

Contents

Preface

'Callsign **GRAY EAGLE**' is the true story of a young man starting out in life and an aircraft carrier and a war.

As my children were growing up, occasionally I would relate an appropriate life story to them from those earlier times. Over time I observed that many of these stories have been an inspiration to my children and others. These are those stories on growing up and taking charge of one's life. "Be responsible for all you do or fail to do". I decided to document the stories and my experiences as I recall them. 'Callsign **GRAY EAGLE**' is a history and a personal story. In many respects it is a storybook of life challenges in the navy and in USS *Ranger* CVA-61 for an electronics and computer technician during the Vietnam War.

When I enlisted in the navy in central Pennsylvania I found that everyone in my boot camp company was from the same area. Jim Hill and I were in the same boot company and two years later in June 1967, taking different paths with different training, were both assigned to the USS *Ranger* CVA-61. Jim was a Photographers Mate (PH) who specialized in taking aerial photos. Having kept in touch, I visited Jim in the summer of 2019 and he graciously allowed me to scan many of the photos seen here from his collection.

John D."Jack" Krebs provided much appreciated and valuable assistance in editing and format discussion. After a short stint in the U.S. Navy at the end of World War II, a career in executive management was launched at International Telephone and Telegraph. That was followed by 25 years in private postsecondary education sometimes as entrepreneur and other times as corporate manager. After earning an MBA he taught in private and public business schools for 20 years. Jack, thank you for introducing me to the English language.

Captain George Bieda, USN Retired, and Mrs. Esther Bieda reviewed the manuscript and encouraged me to continue. George also provided valuable comments on historical events. George, Esther and I graduated from Waipahu High School, Waipahu, Hawaii, Class of 1965.

Getting Started

The First One out of the Hole

In early 1965 I was a senior at Waipahu High School in Waipahu, Hawaii and would be graduating in June. Dad was the Division Safety NCO for 25th Infantry Division at Schofield Barracks. I was an electronics nerd of sorts and a military history buff for sure. I started building radios with a crystal set at age six and by age 10 was fixing radios and at age 13 graduated to repairing TV sets on occasion around the neighborhood. My dad even bought a tube tester for me. By the end of high school, I had been in ham radio for six years, building receivers and transmitters, making my own designs. Built a low frequency radar from some old UHF surplus gear. I also spent time at the Schofield Barracks base library studying and reading military history and strategy books, my other passion.

Our family at our new home in Waipahu, Hawaii, 1962

I always expected to go into the navy because they had the most advanced electronics and were known for the best electronics schools. I wanted to be in a ship working on electronics, I was interested in radio communications and radar. Thought that's all there was. But most of all the Vietnam War was just starting and I wanted to get in while the getting was good. I knew from my military history studies and from growing up in the army that you had to be in the right place at the right time with the right skill set or you didn't get to play. Or, as General Patton would say, "...Shoveling shit in Louisiana", that wasn't for me. My biggest concern in high school was that the war would be over before I could get there.

I was pretty set on the navy but some of the guys at school were talking about the US Army Special Forces and one was taking about the navy Underwater Demolition Team (UDT), first step to Seals. Seals were just getting started. No UDT for me, that involved swimming, I saw the WWII movie. The 'Green Beret' was very interesting to me. As it happened I had some of the Special Forces literature in my room when dad walked in and spotted it. He inquired about it and said he thought I was going navy. I said it was interesting to me, I could be a communications guy in an 'A' Team. He said those guys don't fix radios they throw them away and get another one. "They don't repair anything, they break things". I still thought it was interesting. Dad said, "The army isn't going to make you a lieutenant because you read history books". "Stick with the navy, they have beds, clean sheets, and good food"!

Graduation Day 13 June 1965

A short time later my father came back into my room and said if I was interested he had a friend at work that he could invite for dinner and he would explain all about it and how to get in. I thought that was great and looked forward to the day. I knew recruiters will tell you anything so I was anxious to hear from someone that knows other than dad, of course.

In 1965 there may have been some racism in the army but not much as the army had been integrated for years and the 25th Infantry Division was a combat outfit. In any event there was absolutely no racism in our house, we never thought about such things. We were living in rural Oahu and the only racism I encountered was having a hard time finding an after-school job because I was a Haole (white guy in Hawaii). My friend Michael Suan invited me to join the guys picking pineapple during spring break but I declined that, maybe my father was right I was lazy. During spring break in Hawaii, the boys worked the pineapple fields (good money) and the girls worked in the cannery (good money). No one goes on vacation.

Soon we had a visitor for dinner. I do not remember his name 'SIR' would be close enough, a 6'6" or more big black man, he filled the doorway, Green Beret, full uniform bloused combat boots and all. Five or six rows of ribbons, I asked about the 75 combat jumps ribbon, full on impressive. This was a guy who was definitely not afraid to jump out of an airplane. Daddy introduced him to the family and me, we had a nice dinner.

A very nice gentleman, although I felt sure he could easily stick his finger in your chest and displace your ribcage, should the situation arise. We retired to the living room and he related that my father told him that I was interested in the Special Forces and would be graduating in a few months. I told him that I am interested. He said he could give me a couple pointers; I was all ears. He first asked what position I played on the football team. Clearly at 6'1" and 145 lbs., I was no football player. I told him that I never played football, he next asked if I played any sports at school. I told him I went out for track as a distance runner, leaving out the part that I was just trying to impress a cheerleader that didn't know I existed. He asked if I made the team, I said I didn't, but I did learn how to run pretty well, which was true. Next were questions about martial arts, no, weightlifting, huh. I was beginning to get the idea. He said he could give me some advice about how to get in. First take the next two years, go to junior college, some weightlifting, some martial arts, and a little boxing if I can get into it.

I am thinking to myself 'this is a non-starter', first of all I am leaving home the second I graduate. Like many teens I considered my father to be a little too strict. However in boot camp I would soon find out what discipline was all about. It takes a while longer to realize you have the greatest dad. Besides I figured the war would be over before I could get there if I went to college. My father never discouraged either my brother or me from serving for any reason. Knowing the dangers my father had no problems with my joining any service and was in fact the Army Recruiter that signed my brother as a helicopter pilot the day he turned 18. Jerry's first tour in Vietnam was coincident with my third tour, in two tours Jerry was shot down nine times and has a Silver Star, two DFC's, two Bronze Stars, and at least 48 Air Medals. Jerry was flying at 15 years old. Dad thought we would be the most successful in life if we pursue our passion. Turns out to be true.

I nixed the idea of staying home for Jr. College or anything else and moved on to asking, "can't I just join the army as a soldier designated to Special Forces by the recruiter"? Recruiters will promise anything. He said that could work. "Here is what you are in for". When you graduate from boot and make it through AIT (Advanced Infantry Training) in good standing you will be sent to Fort Bragg, NC for the first of many Special Forces schools.

I thought so far so good, how hard could it be for a kid that camped out in the backyard a couple times, was a good shot with a 22 rifle, and could tell you the order of battle for the Austro-Prussian War of 1866. This is the rest of the story. When the bus arrives at Fort Brag everyone gets off the bus and forms into 12-man teams. I said, ah, "A Teams", he said "not quite". The instructor says, 'pick up a shovel' and each 12-man team starts digging a large hole. At some point when the hole is deep enough the instructor blows a whistle and the first man out of the hole goes on to the world's toughest combat training, the remaining 11 men fill in the hole and get back on the bus headed for assignment to a rifle company in Vietnam. It turns out that only three or four of these remaining 'serious bad asses' out of 100 make it through.

He said in case I was feeling 'lucky' I should consider who I was in the hole with, consider the type of persons that volunteer for this. You have a Golden Gloves boxer or two, Karate Black Belts, Judo, a couple HS or college Fullbacks, and guys that know how to use a shovel for a weapon, get the picture?

After much thought about the moral of that story I decided that life is always being in a hole digging with 11 other guys and that I should equip myself to be the first one out of the hole. The first step for me was doing what I was really good at, electronics, it was the navy for me. Navy Electronics Technician School turned out to be that same hole only at age 17 I had been preparing for 10 years, my hand fit a screwdriver and I knew how to use a soldering iron.

My Dad, Sailor and Soldier

In February 1943 dad drove halfway across Pennsylvania from his home in Lock Haven trying to join the Marine Corp. The Marine Corp was volunteer only in WWII and unbelievable as it may seem in February 1943 they were full up! At least in central Pennsylvania. He got as far as Wilkes-Barre with no luck and turned back, with a stop in Williamsport for one more try. As he sat on the steps of the recruiting station trying to decide what to do next a navy chief came out of the Navy Recruiting Station and began an inquiry. "Trying to join the marines, huh", yes. "They are full up, aren't they", yes. "Is that your car", yes. "You have gas and tires I see", my dad owns a gas station. "So are you good with engines", yes, been working in the garage from a very early age. "We need guys like you in the navy, how would you like to learn diesel engines, how about submarines for excitement".

Dad got an early out from high school in February 1943

Liberty in Honolulu August 1944

and enlisted at 17 years old. He went to boot camp then to eight weeks of Motor Machinist Mate School on diesel engines and generators just like they use on submarines. Did very well in school and made PO3 out of that short school. As a 17-year-old MoMM3, he was assigned to the Destroyer Escort USS *Lovering* DE-39. It has the same diesel electric propulsion as submarines, it turns out he was too young to volunteer for Subs, had to be 18, recruiters will tell you anything.

Dad was promoted to MoMM2 and then Motor Machinist Mate, Petty Officer First Class (E-6) while still 18 years old in USS *Lovering* DE-39, "those were the days". Saw lots of combat in the South Pacific 43-45. In one of the first actions he spoke about the *Lovering* arrived a couple days after the initial beach landing at Tarawa. There were still bodies of marines floating in the water. The *Lovering* was in close to the beach using their 3 Inch guns in direct fire support for the marines. The Japanese were known for sending borders out to ships, actually they did this to abandoned and beached ships close to shore and then attacked from those positions the next day. Dad's "Repel Boarders" station was in the engine room with a 12-gauge shotgun. Later radar was installed on the *Lovering* and they took turns at radar picket duty for the fleet, a favorite target for the inexperienced Kamikaze pilots, go for the first ship you see.

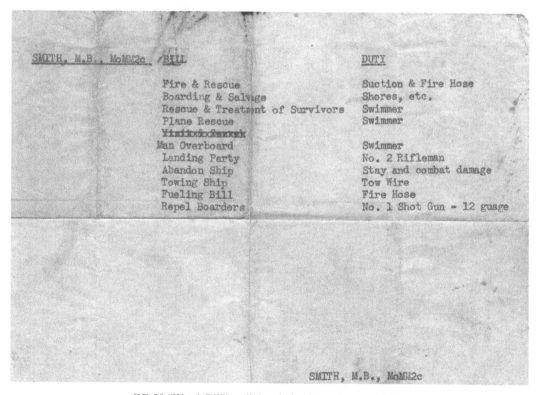

DE-39 "Watch Bill" outlining duties for various conditions

After WWII dad learned to fly on the GI Bill and also started a business. The economy after the war was very slow and he decided to return to the military. He sold his business and paid all his debts. It was 1949 and just before the Korean War. He tried the navy but was told "you have a wife and two kids now, we are still trying to get rid of guys like you", a couple more months and they would have gladly taken him in as a PO1 on the way to chief. As it was, he turned to the army.

In 1949 dad joined the army for an assignment to Officer Candidate School (OCS) at Fort Benning, GA, as a corporal, E-4. But he was dropped from the class and reassigned to train paratroopers. Dad drove an army truck home for lunch sometimes, I loved that. We lived in the trailer park near the jump towers, I could always be found at the fence surrounding the trailer park watching the paratroopers drop from the jump towers. I was in kindergarten there at Fort Benning during part of the Korean War. Economically things were a little rocky at first, but mom and dad managed well, dad did well in the army, retired with 24 years of service including the navy time.

Dad in Korea, 1959

We were next stationed at the New Cumberland General Depot in Pennsylvania. Dad knew nothing of electronics but always encouraged me in electronics, when I was in the fourth grade he built a shed next to our trailer with a workbench for me and my tools. Three years later, at Fort Hood Texas, my shop was in the garage, dad bought a tube tester for me, probably so we didn't need to go to the store to test the tubes for the TV's I was repairing. In Hawaii my shop was in the storage room part of the carport.

Dad Nearing Retirement, summer of 68, at Mary Ellen's wedding

My father taught me to "be responsible for all that I do or fail to do". It was a valuable lesson for life, it served me well.

Mom

Mom grew up in the countryside in McElhattan Pennsylvania right next to Lock Haven where dad grew up. They attended high school together, mom was one year younger. My grandmother on mom's side and my grandfather on dad's side attended the same one room schoolhouse where my great aunt was the teacher. Pennsylvania countryside got to love it.

Mom in the Kitchen, Hawaii 1964

Mom is a very patient and loving person, she very patiently taught me how to draw things, how to observe and visualize details, and how to read. I was pretty good by the first grade. I was the oldest; my sister, Mary Ellen is one year younger, and Jerry is a little less than three years younger.

At many of our duty stations mom worked in the PX and still took care of us. Mom always liked working outside and in the garden as well. Now, as always, at 93 she can often be found outside in the garden.

Enlistment in the US Navy in Hawaii...Well almost

Graduated from Waipahu High School in June 1965 intending to join the navy right away. Dad took me to the recruiting office in Honolulu, as I recall it was a very busy place. We picked up some papers with the intention of filling them out later at home.

One of my best friends in high school, George Bieda, and I were both joining the navy. George was leaving for the US Naval Academy at Annapolis and I was leaving for boot camp. The difference between a 4.0 average and, let's say, less than that. George is now a retired US Navy Captain.

I was working on the enlistment forms when, a couple days later, dad came home from Schofield Barracks and said that since the family was within three months of being transferred he could get authorization and tickets for me to fly to Pennsylvania ahead of the family. This would allow me to spend the summer with my grandparents and Uncle Frank, then join the navy in Pennsylvania after the end of the summer. This sounded great to me so that is what I did. I was anxious to get started but summer with my grandparents had to be all good! And traveling alone from Hawaii to Pennsylvania…great!

Dad was a Sergeant First Class and being transferred from the 25th Infantry Division to recruiting duty, ultimately, to be the new Army Recruiter in Adrian Michigan.

Summer of 65 in Lock Haven, PA

I enjoyed a wonderful summer in Lock Haven Pennsylvania, home of Piper Aircraft, where I and most everyone in the family were born and most of my relatives lived. Uncle Frank had a Piper J3 Cub and we spent many hours flying as the summer weather was mostly great. I got pretty good at slipping the Cub in over the trees and dropping it on the grass beside the runway at Lock Haven airport. Short field landings on grass are great.

Uncle Frank and his Piper J3 Cub, 1965

Also spent some time hanging out with my cousins Chloe Morris and Mike Eyer and my brother Jerry and sister Mary Ellen when they showed up a few months later from Hawaii.

In early September Uncle Ike, Paul Eyer, Lt. Colonel, Local Army reserve Commander, Bronze Star in WWII, ask me about my plans and basically told me 'if you are going to join the navy you need to get busy on the paperwork, they are not going to come to you'. I am sure my dad and mom also wondered if I had a change in plans, I didn't, just my usual procrastination. It was a great summer and it went too fast. Somehow I knew there would never be another.

Enlistment and Boot Camp

I submitted the enlistment forms and the recruiter visited me at my grandparents' house where I was staying. I signed the papers and my parents signed them too as I was 17 and needed their permission. On the eventful day (15 September 1965) when I was to leave, the recruiter came by my grandparents' house in a van to pick me up. We also stopped and picked up several more recruits from other parts of rural Pennsylvania on our way to the recruiting station at Wilkes Barre, PA. I took some more tests and had a physical exam and stayed overnight on the second floor of the recruiting station.

I was getting that feeling of being away from home, not the "fly from Hawaii to Pennsylvania on your own and stay with your grandparents" type of being on your own but the "life is about to change forever" type of being on your own. I was ready.

Service Notes . . .

IN NAVY NOW — Jonathan F. Warner, left, son of Dr. and Mrs. Gilmore Warner, 243 N. Fairview St., and Lynn B. Smith, son of Mr. and Mrs. Morris B. Smith Jr., McElhattan, have enlisted in the Navy and are training at Great Lakes, Ill. Warner, a 1962 graduate of the Lock Haven High School, was put in charge of 40 recruits who left from Wilkes-Barre. He took instruction in the national Red Cross small-craft school and was an instructor for two summers at Waterville, Me. Smith, graduated last June from the Waipahu, Hawaii, High School. His father is an Army sergeant awaiting orders to go to recruiting school.

Amazing what can be found in your parents' scrapbook

The Tonkin Gulf Incident

It looked like war was coming to the Smith family. The Tonkin Gulf Incident occurred in early August 1964 as I was getting ready to attend my senior year at Waipahu High School. We had a good life in Hawaii, it was peacetime and all was well. Suddenly dad came home early from Schofield Barracks and started rooting around in the storage shed for his 'field gear'. I had borrowed the canteen for a hike in the mountains of central Oahu and had lost it. Of course I failed to mention it to dad before this. He said it was OK, he would get another one. Grabbed everything and said goodbye. I didn't know before this, but dad was part of the 'Tropic Lightning Strike Force' of the 25th Infantry division. He spent the next three days sitting next to a C-130 at Hickam Air Force Base before the unit was told to stand down. That was a close one for the family. Dad was transferred a year later to recruiting duty and did not deploy to Vietnam.

Chapter 2

{"x":0}

Chapter 2

Boot Camp

**Recruit Training Command, Great Lakes, Illinois,
16 September 1965**

Camp Barry, Great Lakes (RTC)

The next day a recruit that was not 17 was put in charge of the group of recruits and we all flew to Chicago and then boarded a special bus to Great Lakes Naval Recruit Training Command about 50 miles north of Chicago. We arrived in the middle of the night, maybe 1 or 2AM and were led into a very big hall full of hundreds of double deck bunks, rows and rows. We were told to find one and go to sleep. I did.

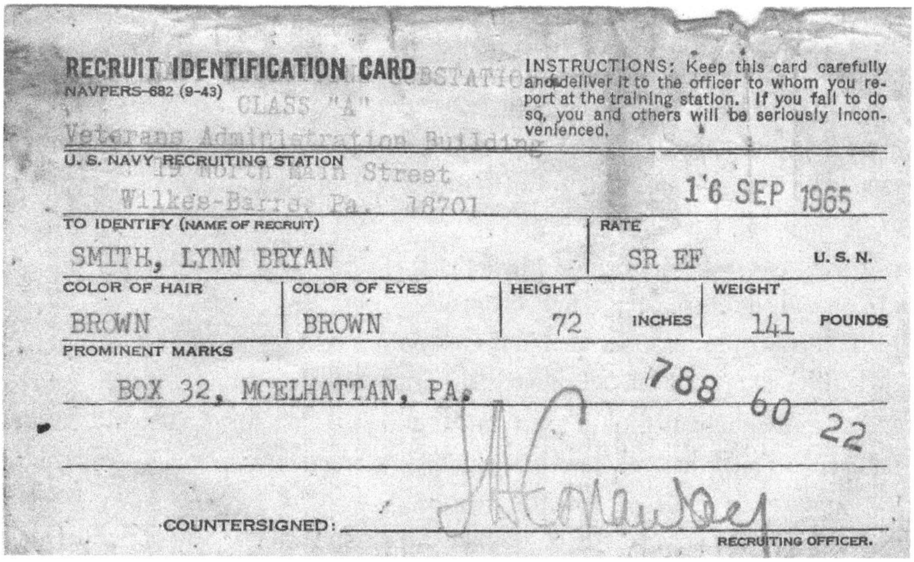

Recruit ID Card

The next morning, they held reveille at 6AM, could have been 5AM not sure now, maybe wasn't sure then. A solid two to four hours sleep, get used to it. The next morning the whole place was full, I couldn't believe it, hundreds and hundreds came in overnight, and they got less sleep. Two men were led away during the night by the Master at Arms (MAA, navy police), because they were caught in bed together. They did tell us one to a bed. I'm guessing they wouldn't have lasted long as sailors anyway considering the times back then. I didn't think about it one way or the other, just surprised at 'how stupid can a person get', in retrospect maybe they wanted out. Just one of the things I never gave a thought to.

A chief got up in front of us and gave a speech. Just like in the movies, some guy was wearing sunglasses at 6AM in the morning and the chief took them off and stepped on them then continued with the speech. Message received. We were at Camp Barry, where you get checked in. I knew there was not going to be anything nice about this. It was raining and after the speech we picked up a Poncho and marched to breakfast, sort of on the marching and sort of on the breakfast. Definite on the foul smell of the Poncho, Ponchos always smell that way, it is the way they are made, smell like vomit.

Over the next three days at Camp Barry we took more tests, more interviews, first round of shots, were issued uniforms, stenciled our name and service number on them. We sent our civilian clothes home in a box; we were in them for almost three days. We were told to memorize our USN seven-digit service number, and the eleven General Orders of a Sentry.

Navy General Orders of a Sentry

1. To take charge of this post and all government property in view.
2. To walk my post in a military manner, keeping always on the alert, and observing everything that takes place within sight or hearing.
3. To report all violations of orders I am instructed to enforce.
4. To repeat all calls from posts more distant from the guard house than my own.
5. To quit my post only when properly relieved.
6. To receive, obey and pass on to the sentry who relieves me, all orders from the Commanding Officer, Command Duty Officer, Officer of the Deck, and Officers and Petty Officers of the Watch only.
7. To talk to no one except in the line of duty.
8. To give the alarm in case of fire or disorder.
9. To call the Officer of the Deck in any case not covered by instructions.
10. To salute all officers and all colors and standards not cased.
11. To be especially watchful at night, and, during the time for challenging, to challenge all persons on or near my post and to allow no one to pass without proper authority.

We were assigned to a company and company commander. I was assigned to Company 501. It turns out the navy had over recruited and had, for the first and last time during the Vietnam War, accepted some draftees. So, the place was crowded. Company flag 501 had not been unfurled since the Korean War and this was only September 17 or 18. We also had 100 men assigned to our company; usually there are 60 men to a company. Later we were to find, to my great delight, that our boot camp experience would be cut short from the customary 11 weeks to only seven weeks. I can't tell you how happy I was about that.

Everyone had to select a religion, it is important because they need to know which Chaplin will be responsible for you. Church service was mandatory in boot camp on Sundays. It was a welcome rest.

Camp Lawrence

" These Boots are made for walking"- Nancy Sinatra

The company commander for Company 501 was ABH1 Wells (Aviation Boatswain Mate, Hydraulic, Petty Officer First Class), remember that name! We marched over to Camp Lawrence; a camp of old WWII wooden 'H' type barracks that had not been used for some time. We were issued a 'piece', a rifle for drill purposes, a Springfield 1903A3 made by Smith Corona. There was no sling on the 'piece' but, no worries; it would never be out of our hands. There was the endless 16 count and 96 count manual-at-arms. You thought the 1903A3 weighs about 10-11 pounds, you would be wrong…feels more like 30 pounds after a couple hours of exercising with it. Each 'piece' had a number stenciled on the side of the stock. We had to memorize that number and, supposedly, were responsible for it. I thought "How could it possibly disappear"?

At Camp Lawrence we were learning to march. The company commander reviewed all the test scores and, I guess because I scored very high, assigned me as a Squad Leader. Within the first minutes on the drill field it became clear that I could not march much less lead a squad in marching. I was relieved of the position as were a couple other nerds like me. So much for the ARI-GCT tests. Apparently, I could be anything I wanted to be in the navy except a Squad Leader in boot camp.

In navy basic training there were no long hikes and no camping out, just a lot of marching. We were issued only two pair of shoes and a pair of ¾ boots we called 'boon dockers'.

The 'Flying Seven'

Seven shots at one time including the blood draw, ugg. 200 of us, of course our sister company went first, they came out looking ragged. They were giving some of the shots with a 'gun'. Put it up to your arm and 'don't flinch' shoot the stuff into your arm, no needle. I almost liked it better until a guy several persons ahead of me flinched and the gun cut his arm. He had blood running down his arm and off his fingertips before you could say ouch. I didn't flinch. You learn these things. Dad would say "Pay attention".

Next came the blood draw. Everyone in a line, hang your arm over the banister, make a fist, and a corpsman inserts a needle in your arm and the syringe begins to fill. Hold your arm out and keep moving, another corpsman about 10 guys ahead was taking them out. No one passed out here, everyone was concentrating on getting down the line to get it taken out! Genius!

Tough luck, buddy...

In the old barracks at Camp Lawrence there was the usual old-style large shower room about like what we had in high school PE but one thing I found that took a little getting used to was the toilet area. There were 20 toilets, ten on each side of the room facing each other and no partitions whatsoever. One morning we were all in a rush, as usual, and as I sat there taking care of business, a guy near me finished up and was pulling up his pants when his toothbrush and toothbrush holder, the kind with a hole at each end, that was in his back pocket fell into the toilet! He paused and then quickly fished it out but the water was already running out the end of the holder! Clean it up, no way to get another one! I was learning to be more careful. Plenty of opportunity to learn from mistakes of others.

More shots

Company 500, our sister company, always got to go first in everything and they would always come out with wild stories about what we were in for. Not the least of which was shots. On what had to be one of the hottest days in early October, about the time I turned 18, some recruits in other barracks were getting sick so they decided everyone would get a Bicillin shot, something a like double dose of Penicillin I am told. We marched to the old wooden building where they were giving this particular shot and waited for our sister company to come out. What a sight, they were all staggering and complaining because the shot is a big one and given in the butt and you have to do a lot of exercise to work it down, so it doesn't knot up. The shot was big and looked like it had the consistency of syrup. What they said was true this time, now it was our turn; we arranged in four rows of 25, a corpsman with a wicker basket full of hypodermic syringes with another corpsman alongside were passing between rows. I was in the third row. The order 'first row drop your pants and bend over', then they went down the row giving the shots and moving from one recruit to another. It was awful, I passed out as they were getting to me in the third row, I never liked shots. When I woke up I was in a chair and the guys in the company were gone. I asked if they gave me the shot already...of course not, they were waiting for me to wake up. Most embarrassing. What a woos! Time to grow up. Happy birthday!

We lost a few recruits at Camp Lawrence, one was a guy I was friends with, he didn't score high and they computed his IQ at 75 and were sending him home, he was sad, wanted to stay. Another guy they sent home wet the bed, he was a married man too, go figure.

Camp Porter

After some time, we sort of graduated from Camp Lawrence and marched over to Camp Porter to the modern, new barracks. Camp Porter was more of the same drill, drill, drill and classes in everything from brushing your teeth to firefighting and shipboard damage control. More shots, of course. I was in a control group that was told to brush our teeth with Crest toothpaste, we would be monitored throughout our career to see what works best…still using Crest and still have all my teeth. The navy never did say when to stop. Often wondered what other brands were being tested, oh well.

More push-ups and manual at arms. Seems like it is always the right time and place for 50 more push-ups. Either individually or as a group.

Swimming tests

I could not swim. At age six or seven the family was at the pool at New Cumberland General Depot, an army base near Harrisburg, PA where daddy was stationed. Someone bumped into me and I fell into the deep end of the pool. I was rescued after I took on a lot of water and never liked the water after that. Mom sent us all, me, Mary Ellen and Jerry, to swimming lessons but I never progressed and hated the lessons. I joined the navy for the electronics not the swimming part. I didn't really think about it. It would seem obvious that a sailor should be able to swim. They have life preservers on ships, don't they, what is the big deal? The navy thought we should all be survival swimmers, in fact, they insisted on it.

The first swimming test

Company 501 and our sister company 500, 200 men in all, were sent to the pool. In the locker room we all changed into our dark blue issue swimming trunks. One guy forgot his trunks and had to wear his skivvies; make one mistake they remember you forever…you don't want that. The PO1 gave a speech and described the test in detail and what was expected. He asked if there was anyone that could not swim. About 40 hands, maybe more, went up along with mine. Then he asked of those who could not swim how many that 'their mothers never had them in more than four inches of bathwater'. Some hands still went up. I kept mine down because I could float, and swim underwater a short distance and I figured if he was talking like that it might not be that bad. I was wrong.

The pool is a full-size Olympic pool with a rope across from one side to the other in the middle essentially cutting the pool in half…the deep end and the shallow end. We would be concerned with the deep end, of course. Near the deepest part but still on the side was a tower. Said to be 12' but it had to be more like 20' because it was so close to the ceiling and when I climbed the ladder there were easily three or four persons on the ladder ahead of me. The pool was enclosed in a building because of the winters, everything is in buildings at Great Lakes, spend a winter there and you know why. The 'non-swimmers' were sent to line up at the shallow end of the pool and watch the others test so they could get an idea of what to do and be horrified. The test involved climbing to the top of the tower and jumping off feet together holding your nose, etc. as if you were abandoning ship, you were then to swim down to the rope and next to the rope across the pool, up the other side, and over the top end back to the tower area where you would be offered a pole and pulled out. The rule was NO touching the rope or the sides or you get to do it over. That was putting it mildly, actually there were instructors along the way, if you touched the side they would pull you out and beat you with a life preserver a couple times and send you to the shallow end of the pool to wait, much yelling involved. I later had a chance to examine the orange life preservers and they were canvas covered wood, ouch! As I am waiting in line to climb the tower the guy two or three in front of me was telling everyone to relax and not worry too much, he was a lifeguard for a couple summers, assured us we would be OK. I was almost next at the top of the tower, scared like hell, when he jumped and appeared to flounder getting his direction, the instructors yelled at him to grab the pole. That means they will pull you out right now, he didn't grab the pole so they struck him with it to get his attention and he went unconscious and went under. One of the instructors jumped in and pulled him out. So, the process was delayed a little while they gave him first aid. Soon it was my turn. I didn't have a chance and I knew it. I jumped after being twice ordered to jump, the second time was loud, I went down, floundered a bit, grabbed the pole and went to the shallow end with the non-swimmers and the former lifeguard.

After the test was over and everyone else went to the locker room it was the turn of the non-swimmers to test. Sure enough, most of us could not swim; the lifeguard did pass the second time, I am sure with a headache.

Swimming lessons

Swimming lessons were held at the same pool as the first test, there were at least three pools as I was to find out soon enough. It was organized much the same way as any swim class but with the little navy extra. At the shallow end was the beginning swimmers, the instructors were very mean and I don't mean maybe. They were a little nicer as you progressed toward the deep end. Another little thing, it seems like there were ice cubes in the water at the shallow end, really cold, but as you progressed the water was warmer. I saw what was happening and since I could float after a fashion and swim underwater, I put myself into the floating part. Swimming lessons were given during the little time you had to write letters and polish shoes, etc. In three days I learned to backstroke my way around the pool...well sort of, good enough. The instructor at the tower this time was very nice "now gentlemen this is not a hard thing to do, just take your time, I am here to help you", etc. I jumped off the tower and backstroked my way to successfully pass the test. Talk about motivation, I haven't had to swim since, I do not do pools.

The second swimming test

THE AMERICAN NATIONAL RED CROSS

This certifies that

Lynn B. Smith

has completed satisfactorily a course in
BASIC SURVIVAL SWIMMING
and has met all test requirements

OCT 1 1985

Alfred W. Cromwell
National Director
Safety Services

Proof that I can swim,
still 17 years old

The second test involved jumping into the pool with your clothes on, pulling off your dungaree pants, tying the end of each leg in a knot, swing them over your head (they must be wet, no problem with that) to capture air in the legs and using that as a life preserver swim to the other side. Swimming back using your white hat out in front of you as a float board, works well, keep kicking. All survival techniques using your shipboard working uniform. To save time and drowning they gave us pants that were already tied and wet. This one was easy. Almost fun.

The third swimming test

This last test had a large pool with the rope across it at the halfway point and a large raft in the water on the far side. The idea was to treat the area from the rope to the raft as being on fire, so swim to the rope, then swim underwater to the raft and come up with your arms making a big splash as to open a fire free area and get hauled into the raft. I did this one, no problem.

No spitting!

In boot camp there is <u>NO</u> spitting. No doesn't mean maybe or when necessary or if you are sick, it means NO! Of course someone will always put this to the test with the usual unsurprisingly predictable results. It was cold, our company was lined up outside the galley, chow hall for you army folks, waiting for our turn to march in and get in line inside. We were all bundled up in our heavy Pea Coats when one guy coughs up a large lugie and looks around and then spits it on the pavement, at least is was not on the Admiral's grass. It was an ugly green. Unfortunately a chief saw him do it and came right over and ordered him to get down and eat it up! My dad is an Army Sergeant and I already knew not to spit on the ground but now that was confirmed!

Another lesson I learned at home is never put your hands in your pocket. I watched as others learned that lesson at 50 push-ups per lesson. It is a military axiom that pockets are not for hands!

Back to routine training

It was getting colder and we marched a lot in the large drill halls that resembled airplane or blimp hangars. These were purpose built to be drill halls. Marched to the music of Souza.

An interesting thing happened toward the end of recruit training. Things were getting easier and the company commander was treating us better. Then one Saturday he came in and did not stay long, the next day he didn't come in at all, for the first time ever we were on our own so to speak. During the day a regular navy seaman shows up at the barracks. This is not legal; no regular navy personnel are ever allowed near the 'boots'. He calls everyone together like he was sent there but I knew better when he started talking. Daddy was an army sergeant and I had heard of these tricks already. So as the story goes, Mr. Wells was in an accident with his motorcycle and was in financial trouble because of the accident and was going to lose something, sad story, etc., etc. But it would be a great help to the 'old company commander', who has been so nice to us in our last days, if we each kicked in $5. Many seemed eager to pitch in. Of course, after he said his piece I just had to speak up. I told everyone this was the oldest scam in the book and to keep their money in their pockets. I think the take was pretty slim because of me.

The next day I was called into the CC's office located at the end of the barracks floor and surrounded by glass with a door. Wells chased the company clerk out so we would be alone, and he asked me what my 'piece' number was. Our de-milled 1903 Springfield drill rifle was referred to as a 'Piece' as in 'Drill Piece'. I rattled it off. I was standing at attention as he told me that was incorrect that my piece number was such and such, which was one of the pieces in the rack that had a broken stock and was not assigned to anyone. 'The cost of the broken stock would be deducted from my pay'. Standing at attention with no one in the room I told him that if he did that, I would report him to the battalion commander and would go as high as I had to get him a Courts Martial, I had 99 witnesses. I told him I was the son of an army sergeant and knew what the hell was going on. It was a big risk because I didn't want to get set back and didn't know how high the scam went but I guessed it was just him because of the sleazy seaman. I was dismissed and never heard another word about it. I became off-limits to punishment it seems, but we were about to graduate anyway.

Getting 'set back' is a constant fear for anyone in boot camp because the company commander could have you sent back to another company to repeat some of the training for the most minor of infractions. This would mean a longer stay at boot camp, something no one wanted, especially me. If one really screwed up one could get sent to the disciplinary barracks' known as the "Mouse House", or "Mickey Mouse". Life there was said to be very tough. Unpleasant doesn't begin to cover it. We had a mouse house guy dropped into our company; he was THE most squared away guy ever. He admitted to me that he was a major 'give a shit' hard case before the mouse house. Now a gentleman sailor of the first order. It is all about 'attitude adjustment'.

Service Week

Near our last week in recruit training there is a long navy tradition called 'Service Week'. This is where you get to do a job just like you would at your next command. Usually service week is two weeks long but since our training period was cut short we had only one week...darn! My service week job was working in the galley, food service. I was assigned to the milk machines, cleaning the gleaming stainless-steel machines and changing the milk cartons when they were empty. Actually an easy job as galley jobs go. When you work in the galley once you sort of never want to go back. I was thinking, I wonder if I could get to like it in time...NO! My BoonDockers, 3/4 high work boots, never took a shine again after Service Week, some kind of grease or something.

33 years later my daughter Jane had service week in this very same galley. I thought hahaha, bet your BoonDockers never take a shine again... I was wrong, I should have known, Jane was assigned as the storekeeper in the galley and never left a comfortable desk.

Graduation

It was already cold the second week in November when we graduated. We marched into the great drill hall to the music of Souza, the guests were all there in the bleachers and the ceremony went forward without a hitch. Little did I imagine that 33 years later, almost to the day, my daughter Jane would be standing within feet of where I was standing, third row, second company from the end, and I would be in the bleachers!

Boot leave, a real sailor now, I packed my seabag and waited on the famous train station platform in my peacoat for the train to Chicago, then on to Adrian Michigan to visit dad, mom, brother Jerry and sister Mary Ellen.

For the next two years everything I owned in this world would fit in my 'sea bag'.

Great bunch of guys, all from central Pennsylvania. I am the tall skinny kid, last row fourth from the right
Jim Hill is forth row, sixth from the right, with glasses

CHAPTER 3

ET School

Electronics Technician School
Great Lakes Naval Training Center (NTC), Great Lakes, Illinois
November 1965

After the short 'Boot' leave at mom and dad's new home in Adrian, Michigan I reported back to Great Lakes, but this time it was the Naval Training Center (NTC) side where many service schools were located. I was reporting to the electronics technician (ET) school, or so I thought. This was about mid-November, historically about the time the battle of the Ia Drang Valley (movie, We Were Soldiers) was taking place in Vietnam.

US Naval School Electronics Technician, Building 520

The test

I went through the check-in process and was all set up in a barracks, etc. I was told to report to a certain building the next morning at 07:30, plenty of time to have breakfast first.

When I arrived at the building I was ushered into this very large room filled with tables and chairs and told to have a seat. I would say there were about 600 guys, including some Waves, seated when the room was finally full. While everyone was arriving, I asked a petty officer who seemed to be in charge what we were doing here. He explained that we were going to be given a test, and that test would determine if we would go to Electronics Technician (ET) or Machinist Mate (MM) or telephone repair (IC) or Electrician Mate (EM) school. I explained that maybe I was in the wrong place because I was already designated to ET school.

Yes, I spoke the words, 'my recruiter said' so he looked at my card and it was printed with letters 'EF' which apparently means 'electrical field', I was in the right place...one more test. I wasn't worried because I aced every electronics test they gave so far. "I been doing this since I was six", furthermore I'm a genius, right?

Two guys sitting across the table from me were chatting it up. I started to talk with them and found out they were both actually graduate electronics engineers and were on retainer from IBM and would return to their jobs when they got out of the navy in less than four years. They did not want to be officers, they just wanted to get out, it was the time of Vietnam...join the navy instead of being drafted into the army. I was to see a lot of that. In any event I thought that was two seats in the class filled, I later found out they went to the 'accelerated' course which only takes a couple months for those who already know it all...like graduate engineers.

Several guys were at the end of the next table, all talking to one guy. I thought he looked familiar, I remembered seeing his photo in one of the popular electronics magazines around 1964 or so. He built a satellite in his back yard in Florida. In those days everyone was crazy about space.

As I looked around the room I came to realize the navy had collected a bunch of geniuses from all over the country. It seemed I was just another one of the crowd!

I should mention that in my senior year in high school when I took second year algebra I knew the teacher (I think I had Mrs. Kim) would not fail a senior so I mostly did no homework. I did pay attention in class and when it came my turn to explain a problem to the class Annabel Watasaki slid her paper over to me so I would not be embarrassed. Generally, I felt like I could not factor the simplest equation!

The test papers were distributed and we were told to start, I believe it was a timed test. This was not the electronics test I took before, this was awful. It seemed like most of the questions were right out of second year algebra, quadratic equations, imaginary numbers, the works! I was lost, I thought I would end up an electrician. It turns out I passed by one question, whew! I was assigned to ET school class 23.

Class 23

Since WWII the goal of the navy ET school is to provide an EE college education crammed into 36 weeks, 'don't need no English, history or civics', no term papers, and no parties. The US Navy ET School is one of the top-rated electronics trade schools in the US. It has to be because the navy has the most sophisticated equipment in the military and you will be at sea with it and no one to turn to. No 'group think' here.

Class 23 started with 140 men and women geniuses divided into three classes,

23A, 23B and 23C, I was in 23B. If you don't keep up, you are gone. The navy is quick to determine that you are not "getting with the program". They have a place for you in the fleet swabbing a deck and chipping paint on a destroyer somewhere. Lots of destroyers in the navy.

This is ET-A school, 'A' school is the basics and a lot more, 'B' school is very advanced, they built their own vacuum tubes and transistors, real science, 'C' schools are advanced schools for particular equipment types and systems.

A buddy and I just starting ET School, NTC Great Lakes, rare warm day, no snow on the ground yet, November 65. Behind the old WWII 'H' Type barracks where we were billeted all through ET School

Day one, we went into Ohms Law and by the end of the week we were through Kirchhoff's Current Theories. At the end of that first week and every one of the first ten weeks a test was given and if you did not pass you were gone, no retakes, no extra study, no excuses, just immediate transfer. By week ten we were into power supplies with labs, I was eating it up. I did have to pay extra attention to the math for a couple weeks...'J factors' (imaginary numbers), quadratic equations, etc. but I got it.

By week ten we dropped 95 of the genius', only 45 of us were left to finish the course. Apparently, the navy figured out that if you made the first ten weeks you had what it takes to complete the course. After week ten if you failed a test you were given a second chance after a good talking to. Then if you failed again you could be up on charges, UCMJ Article 15, yes it could be a crime. I guess they figured you were distracted with a girlfriend somewhere, look for restriction to the barracks and mandatory study after school. The fleet was still waiting...you could be an ET or a paint chipper, still had the choice. I never failed a test.

For those who know about ET School sometime in 1966 the first 10 to 12 weeks of ET-A school were separated and renamed BE&E (Basic Electricity and Electronics). These first ten weeks of electrical theory, as it turns out, are common to many Rates in the navy (ET, DS, EM, IC, AT, AQ, etc.). Later I was to have DS's working for me that just went to BE&E and then on to DS-A and DS-C schools without ET school. Generally they were not as effective when it came to troubleshooting actual electronics but OK with computers.

The rest of the course would be intensive study of amplifiers, tubes, solid state, RF, microwave, waveguides, radar, mercury vapor thyratrons, power supplies, radio receivers and transmitters, synchros, servos, amplidynes and test equipment, we built our own oscilloscope, an OS-8. Troubleshooting and repair methods were in there too.

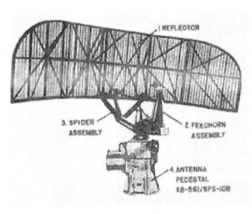

SPS-10 Radar Antenna Assembly

We were all taught the AN/SPS-10 surface search radar in ET-A school because it was a good lesson in radar and there was one on every ship in the navy at the time. It was an early 1950's radar but it had everything. Magnetron, klystron, wave guides, horn, dish, synchros, servos, amplidynes, receiver circuits, SPA-8 PPI operator display, it was all there.

The navy has the best training aids ever. In one class on synchro and servo control systems we had a complete SPS-10 radar antenna in the center of the classroom, mount, servo motors, big dish and all on a large wooden table on castors wheels connected to the controls by a long cable.

One day when we went to lunch someone set the antenna to sweep back and forth and released the wheel locks. When we all returned from lunch the whole assembly had made its way around the room and pushed all the desks to the sides of the room. The instructor acted like nothing happened, guess he saw that one before. Maybe that was the lesson.

The barracks, food, watch standing

The old WWII wooden 'H' type barracks we stayed in were steam heated, nice and cozy warm in the winter. They were divided into two sides each with an upper and lower floor with restrooms, offices, and washrooms between sides. I was usually in lower east. Each quadrant was laid out with dividers that provided for two double bunks spaced three feet apart with a single table and chair at the end and blocked by four lockers, two on each side. This formed a nice little informal cubicle for four guys.

Galley 409, ET School, NTC Great Lakes

The food was great. It was the first time I ate 'Honey Dew' melon, didn't know what it was before, guess I led a sheltered life.

One of the duties was 'watch standing', the navy's version of guard duty. Because we were in school the middle of the night watches were only two hours otherwise they were the standard four hours and suspended during school hours.

Cleaning the barracks was also an assigned duty, usually to the lowest rank, made me want to go up in rank faster. I did everything I could to get to seaman, E-3, as fast as I could. It was more money too. I went from $72 to $93 per month, but we were paid twice a month, so that was nice.

The weather

The 'Storm Watch' was a good one to have unless it was snowing! In the winter of 65-66 at Great Lakes we had snow that drifted to 12 to 15 feet in a couple days then the temperature fell to -20F (too cold to snow). The instructors could not get to school and we were all ordered to stay in the barracks. The snow covered the first story of the barracks completely up to the second floor. The job of the Storm Watch was to shovel snow and keep the sidewalks open. It was like the trenches of WW1, 12-foot-high walls. Get a shovel full and throw it as high as you can...at 2AM to 4AM in the morning! Wonderful!

The man who serviced the soft drink machine in the barracks could not get there many times when the weather was bad, so he left stacks of cokes next to the machine and if you wanted one you just gave a dime to the Barracks Watch in the office and they put it in a box for him, the honor system. The issue was the cokes were warm, so to cool them off we opened a window and put the coke between the window and the screen for about 10 minutes. We tested this and found on one occasion the bottle broke in 20 minutes...that's cold!

Homework, notice the slide rule, handheld calculators were not invented yet

Karate Joe

One night I relieved the watch to assume my 2-4AM barracks watch and the guy I relieved said "I guess you will be on until 6AM". I asked why, and he pointed out that my relief for the 4-8 watch was "Karate Joe" and nobody wakes him up, they just take his watch because everyone is afraid to wake him. I had heard of Karate Joe, he was in another quadrant from me. I was unimpressed, I heard he was put on report once for putting his hand through a plate glass window demonstrating his 'Karate'. There is always one. This was a challenge for me! I had two hours to think up something. On my roving patrol I walked past his bunk and saw with my flashlight he was rolled up in a blanket on the top bunk, feet out toward the passageway. When it was time to wake him for his watch I quietly approached his bunk and in one quick move grabbed his feet and rolled him out of the top bunk. As he was rolled up in a blanket and could not get loose, he fell from the top bunk and hit the table and chair with a loud crash, it had to hurt! He got up mad as hell, I shined the flashlight in his eyes and told him it was time to get up for his watch. Word got around, there was a complete lack of sympathy for Karate Joe. I heard Karate Joe was a light sleeper on nights when he had the watch.

UDT (Underwater Demolition Team) recruiting ET's

A buddy in the barracks, former lumberjack, not an ounce of fat, told me of a posted notice, the navy was looking for ET volunteers for UDT/SEAL training. At that time SEALs were new, you went UDT (Underwater Demolition Team) first, then maybe SEAL. He was going to try out and wanted me to come and watch, I told him he was crazy...you have be able to swim like a fish. I went to the first tryout to watch, what else is there to do on a Saturday at Great Lakes? I sat in the bleachers. A SEAL lieutenant organized everyone into five groups, one group at a time will run with him and not to get ahead of him. Not to worry, no one was going to get ahead of this Olympian as he ran all five groups ragged and was not even breathing hard. I went back to the barracks, didn't want to watch what might be next...swimming! I cannot remember if my friend was selected.

Orders

About week 28 or 29, maybe earlier, we submitted our 'dream sheets', or request for orders for assignment upon graduation. I put in for 'any ship any station Western Pacific' because I wanted to go to Vietnam. I was 18 and it was the only war in town. As a secondary I put in Hawaii, of course I knew they would never send me there, so I figured my first choice was a 'no brainer'. Never underestimate the US Navy, it turns out everyone in the class, to the man, put in for the east coast or the Sixth Fleet, in the Mediterranean. When the orders came in everyone was going to Vietnam...except one...me, I was assigned to the Naval Communication Station, San Juan, Puerto Rico. It was an island! Not only not Vietnam but not even sea duty! I wanted an aircraft carrier; it was my dream. It is possible the main reason I got that assignment is that I was a 'kiddy cruiser', that is, since I enlisted at 17 years old my enlistment was three years instead of four, I only had two years left at this point.

I thought 'no problem' I can just arrange a swap with someone in the class. I went to the chief and then to the lieutenant and was told in no uncertain terms "NO"! They reasoned that I was selling my really choice orders to someone in the class. I said they could pick the person, but they only said it was prearranged that whoever got my orders would pay! What an imagination! The agreed upon price was only $200! Just kidding.

Extending my enlistment

Back in the barracks I was probably looking very dejected over the whole state of affairs. One of the guys I knew only from the barracks asked me what was wrong, and I told him the whole sad story. He said he knew how to get out of the orders, I was interested. It was simple extend your enlistment for another school, that would break the orders and I could have another shot at orders after the second school. Surely, I would go to Vietnam after that. But what school? I already attended the top electronics school...or so I thought. Anyway, more schools would only delay me, what if the war was over before I got there!

He was in the DS-A school for Data Systems Technician...computers. I didn't even know the navy had computers aboard ship, at that time it was a well-kept secret. He took me over to the school for a look around. This school was for 'card carrying' members only, in other words security clearance required, you can't get in without an escort. I was impressed, little did I know it was only the training computers, I thought 'this is for me'! It was at the end of DS-A school before I was allowed to know what the navy really had on ships; I was totally flabbergasted!

It turns out you need to be in the top 10% of your ET school class to apply for the DS school. I had no idea where I placed, didn't care up to now, was just having a ball like a kid in a toy store. Turns out I was in the top 15% but they decided to waive the standing and let me in. Probably because I was willing to extend my enlistment by three years to six years for others the extension would have been only two years for the six-year commitment.

I signed the extension papers and was slated to start DS-A school right after ET-A.

CHAPTER 4

Data Systems Technician 'A' School Computers July 1966

DS-A school was a 10-week course with a new class starting every 5 weeks. It was all about the basics of computers and logic. The first week was logic gates, Boolean algebra, and the usual so much more. It was difficult to get a grip on everything after the fun of being knee deep in communications and radar. I failed the first week test! I was told not to fail another one. The second week, can you imagine, we were already into computer architecture and programmed instruction execution. What the hell is memory? I thought I was just starting to get a grip but failed the second test.

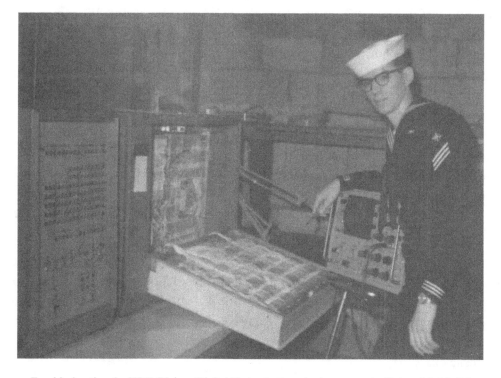

Troubleshooting the UDT (Univac Digital Trainer) otherwise known as the Univac Model 422

You're out!...or...Let's make a deal

I was called to the office and the lieutenant told me I was out! I was very disappointed because I wanted to complete the course. It was just getting interesting. So, I said I wanted my three-year extension back if I wasn't going to get the school. I told him I was really starting to catch on and that Boolean algebra was a mind twister at first. He said, "You are not cut out for computers"! He finally agreed to give me another chance but if I failed any more tests I would be transferred immediately to the Fleet as an Electronics Technician and the extension would stay in place. I agreed. Then he said I cannot go back to my class and will have to wait three weeks for the next class, and he would make sure I got **the worst jobs he could find for the next three weeks!** I was "going to work"! Sometimes things happen for a reason, if I had stayed in that class chances are excellent that I would have been assigned to the USS Forrestal when it blew up off the coast of Vietnam on 29 July 1967. Some of my first classmates were, I will describe one later.

Get ready to work!...or...A charmed life begins

He wasn't kidding, I was ordered to report in my dungaree work uniform to an old WWII barracks that was being 'reconditioned'. I showed up in the morning as ordered in my nice new and hardly ever worked in dungaree work uniform, clean, pressed and spic and span. When I walked in I saw the whole place was being torn apart, dirt flying everywhere. Somebody asked me who I was, and I said "Smith, LB, ET-SN", they were expecting me. I knew it would be a preverbal 'shit storm' when I saw a First-Class Petty Officer covered in dirt raining down as he was tearing into some rusty pipes from WWII. The PO1 told me it was time to get to work, after all I had been standing there almost 60 seconds, and hand him a large pipe wrench that was covered in dirt and grime, you get the picture. Just as I reached for the wrench a seaman dressed in whites, an office type, came in and said he was looking for Smith ET-SN, I said that was me. He said, "Change of orders, go back to the barracks and change into your white uniform and report to the ET-C school for duty immediately". It turns out I was the only person available who's security clearance was already approved so I spent the next three weeks at the ET-C school checking badges at the front desk, they were all classified schools. The beginning of a charmed life.

The second time through the DS-A school I felt like I knew this stuff forever, having so much fun. I loved troubleshooting computers. Our computer in 'A' school was the 'Univac Digital Trainer' or UDT also known as the Univac 422. I was second in the class after a guy who never missed a question on any test, probably from kindergarten. There is always one, left front row in the class photo, sharp as a tack, reenlisted from Yeoman. He was a good technician.

Graduation, Next Stop Mare Island

Upon graduation I was transferred to Mare Island, California to attend DS-C schools, my specialty was to be NTDS Data Communications. I was very happy about that, radios and computers!

Back Row, Fourth from the right again, only a smaller group this time

All of this class was headed for Mare Island. Some would be in the Data Communications class with me, NEC 1617. Some in Computers and some in Digital Displays and associated equipment.

Greg Boyd, back row on the right, and I went to the USS *Ranger* together. I made first class before he did, but Greg stayed in and made chief. Kestner is on the back row far left, as a DS2 he would be one of my gang at Dam Neck four years later.

CHAPTER 5

DS-C School

Data Systems Technician 'C' Schools
Mare Island, California, November 1966

I was designated an NEC-1617 and would be trained on Data Communications equipment for the Naval Tactical Data System (NTDS), very advanced shipboard automated Combat Information Center (CIC). Hot stuff, I was very excited.

US Navy 'C' schools are advanced schools on specific equipment, in this case too. During this intensive seven months of Data Transmission 'C' schools I was trained on the AN/USQ-20 computer from Univac, NTDS Link-11 data link with the AN/SRC-16 HF radio system and AN/SSQ-29 Data terminal from Collins Radio, and the NTDS Link-4A data link with the AN/SRC-17 UHF radio from Manson Labs and AN/SSW-1 data terminal from Western Electric. Very detailed and fast-moving schools. All these equipment's and the schools were classified. Card carrying members only.

CP-642A NTDS Standard Computer with front doors open
Big Computers now

At the time I went through 'Data Transmission' school the navy was only training 30 persons a year, three classes of 10, on this equipment. This would later account for a desperate shortage of trained DS's as the navy was expanding rapidly on the success of NTDS on combat ships. One student in our class for a time was a Naval Officer from the Guatemalan Navy. No photos of the graduating classes from this school.

Of course, there are many other components to the NTDS system and many others were being trained on those, it was a busy school of the very latest high technology.

An early Univac brochure, the CP-642A (Univac 1206 Computer) and associated components of the NTDS System, the computer is six feet tall

Very few persons dropped out of the 'C' schools, partly because we worked with the few guys that were not catching on well and partly because we were the crème of the ET classes. But if you failed here you just went to sea as an ET which would put you above most of the paint scraping and chipping but not all, even as a DS, I was to find out later.

The AN/SRC-16 Radio Set for NTDS Link-11
Ranger had an extra bay of eight more 6-30MHz antenna multi-couplers for nine bays in all

Classes went on full swing. The NTDS School was in a large building complex that used to be a hospital before WWI and through WWII. The FTM School, 'Fire Control

Technician Missile', was up on the hill behind us. Lots of technology at Mare Island. I continued to hone my skills with the floor buffer and cleaning the head (restroom). I noticed the toilet paper was brown like butchers' paper but a little thinner and shinier, looked at the box we were taking it from and noticed we were still using up the 1945 paper. Still good...for young people.

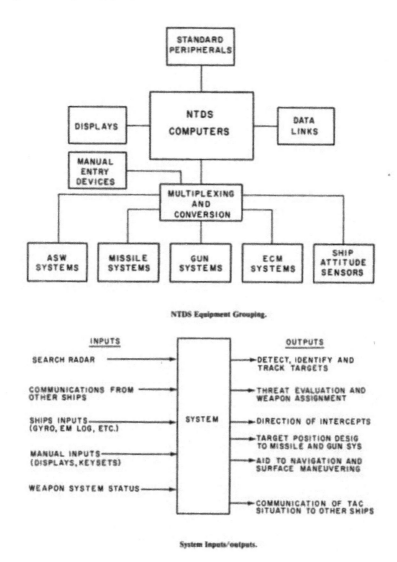

NTDS Equipment Grouping.

System Inputs/outputs.

Block Diagram typical of the NTDS Shipboard System

The classes at Mare Island went well, lots of fun again learning all about new stuff I never knew existed and most of the rest of the world didn't know existed either.

We were all billeted in Barracks 930 near the gate to the road leading to the ammunition magazines. When I was stationed there the gate was locked, no entry permitted. Later I visited Mare Island when it was closed as a naval base and turned over for civilian use. Down that road was a cemetery with many graves from many ships. Some research, without revisiting the cemetery shows that many civilians and brave sailors and marines from many ships are interred there from the Civil War through about 1930 or so. Notably the granddaughter of Francis Scott Key is also interred there. Historical place to visit.

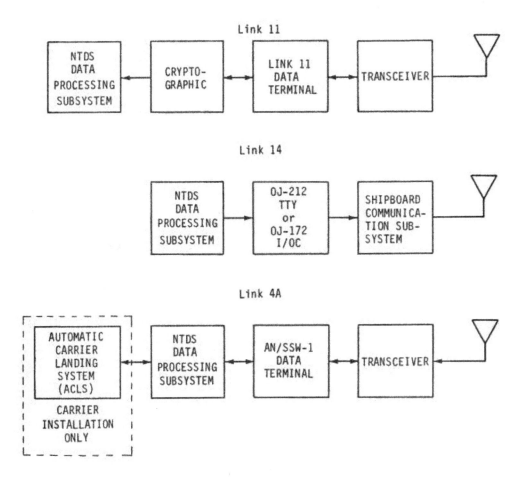

Data Link Systems for the Naval Tactical Data System

Link-11 is ship to ship and ship to the marines Marine Tactical Data System (MTDS) ashore and to the E-2 Hawkeye Airborne Tactical Data System (ATDS). Link-14 is a secure teletype link to non-NTDS ships so they can remain up to date regarding track information, etc. Link-4A is the direct data link to combat aircraft like the A6 Intruder, A7 Corsair II, and F4J Phantom II.

Across the road from Barracks 930, near the pier, was the PBR (Patrol Boat River) training center. The Vietnam War was in full swing and they were training a lot of 'brown water sailors'. Someone said they were looking for a few ET's, of course we were past being allowed to join that group. Anyway, I woke one night about 1AM and looked out to see them all running down to the water in their swimming trunks for a little midnight swim in the Bay. It was around March in the SF Bay, nothing tropical about it. Swimming and cold didn't do it for me, bad combination, count me out.

The classes were graded on a curve except ours because we had 'Scotty' who sat in class, knitting, never opened a book but aced every test. I worked with Scotty in the lab and thought he would not do well on a ship, could not troubleshoot well, his 'hand did not fit a screwdriver', he was not 'one' with the gear.

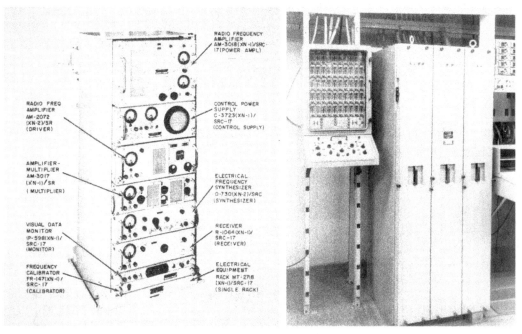

The AN/SRC-17 UHF Radio Set for NTDS Link4-A, data link to A6, A7, and F4J aircraft

The AN/SSQ-29 NTDS Link-11 Data Terminal Set with control console, later I was trained on the newer AN/USQ-36 NTDS Data Terminal Set when *Ranger* had one installed for Link-21

Graduated well up in my class, all ten of us did well, bright class. Professionals all by this time. Ready for the fleet, "the new breed of sailor", computers at sea.

Mare Island Blue

While I was at Mare Island for seven months attending the NTDS data communication schools I discovered they had a rifle team. In fact, two rifle teams, Mare Island Gold and Mare Island Blue. Sounded good to me so I checked into it and was accepted to start with Mare Island Blue, second stringers, just before a shoot against the army at Fort Ord. I had experience with the M1 Garand prior to joining the navy but didn't get a chance to shoot with the team before the army competition. The team was shooting the National Match M1 Garand in 30-06 of course.

The day of the army competition it was cold and overcast at Fort Ord and it was a long ride there in the back of the van. Being second stringers we were in the cold and dank trench down-range pulling targets all morning while 'Gold' shot. By the time we got to shoot it seems the army was ahead of 'Gold' and the chief no longer cared how we second stringers shot. I was having trouble getting the sights adjusted at the 50 and 100-yard ranges. It had been two years since I shot an M1 at my grandfather's house during the summer in Pennsylvania. Finally I was getting the hang of it and started to do better. At the 600 Yard range, I remember it being 600 but some say 500 was the limit, the bull's eye is a 36-inch round dot on a 3' by 3' page. At this long range we were shooting prone, laying down, of course with iron sights, no scope. I got the range and laid them in shot after shot. I shot near the top for the day at that range. Too bad I didn't do well any time before that, ended up scoring near the bottom overall.

After that I never had time to make any other meets. Isn't it always true, second stringers pull targets? Stick with what you know.

27 years later (1994-1995) my eldest son, Jay, deployed to the Mediterranean in the USS *Nassau* LHA-4 as a Marine Scout Sniper. Jay shoots real well, I can't outshoot him either.

Orders

Coming out of 'C' school the navy didn't bother to ask where we wanted to go. NTDS is a shipboard system, never mind asking for a shore billet. Professionals now, everyone was going where they were needed period. Next stop Tonkin Gulf.

I was happy, finally I was going to Vietnam and in an aircraft carrier, how good is that!

CHAPTER 6

Assigned USS *Ranger* CVA-61
Callsign **GRAY EAGLE**

Finally, an Aircraft Carrier, careful what you wish for!

"The Sea stalks the unwary and relentlessly pursues the careless", author unknown.

The Big Fleet Attack Carriers

In the late 60's there were two types of fleet aircraft carriers. The USS *Ranger* was a Forrestal class CVA, CV for aircraft carrier and A for 'Attack Aircraft Carrier'. When deployed the big CVA's like *Ranger* usually had a crew of 4,500 to 5,000 men, no women at the time, with about 90 large aircraft of all types and 4 1/2 acres of flight deck. About 2,500 men were 'Ships Company' assigned to the ship, we call this the 'Black Shoe Navy' and about 2,500 men belonged to the various air wing units, the aircraft were theirs, this is referred to as the 'Brown Shoe Navy'. All steeped in naval history. We in the black shoe navy just called them 'Airedales'. The smaller carriers were known as CVS's, "S" for Anti-Submarine Warfare. Many of the CVS's were actually large Essex class carriers from WWII like the USS *Yorktown* and the USS *Hornet* but nowhere the size of *Ranger*.

NAS Alameda, Transit Barracks:

I was authorized a short two week leave in Michigan and Pennsylvania during which I managed to roll my brother Jerry's 1965 VW Beetle. Totaled it in style, rolled side over side and end over end, ended up laying on the passenger side, had to roll down a window to get out. I was not hurt. Jerry was OK with it because he bought a new VW Carman Ghia. This evaporated my pre-navy saving so I was starting navy life clean.

Now a Third-Class Petty Officer, I reported, as ordered, to Naval Air Station, NAS Alameda to catch the USS *Ranger*, CVA-61, that was home ported there. I was told on checking in that I had 'missed ships movement' which is a serious offense in the navy. I quickly pointed out that I reported three days early and it was not my fault that the ship decided to leave even earlier without me! The issue was dropped. *Ranger* had left for the San Diego area for training with various air wing units, I was to find out later this is the worst time on a carrier...playing flight deck to mixed squadrons not your own. Got to train those pilots but it is not routine for the crew, guys on leave, the galley not fully manned, etc. Life at sea during stateside training periods is not the greatest.

I asked if they could fly me down to catch the ship in San Diego but they said there would be more crewmembers coming in and they will just hold everyone in the 'transit barracks' until the ship gets back, SOP. So, I was to endure the 'transit barracks' for the next two weeks. So much for checking in early, no good deed goes unpunished.

Naval Air Station, Alameda. 1) Small Navy Exchange, 2) Transit Barracks
3) Enlisted Club, 4) Marine Barracks, 5) Waves Barracks

Because I was a third-class petty officer I was put in charge of about 20 seaman for work details. I just knew the old Chief Boson' that ran the transit barracks was going to be trouble when I saw him run out of his office to stop and dress down an Ensign for not having his 'cover' (hat) on. The young Ensign was distracted carrying papers and going somewhere, had his cover under his arm, the chief gave him hell. Even if you are a chief you just don't talk to Officers that way. Now everyone knew if the chief said jump, you will just jump right now, never mind asking silly questions like 'how high'.

My assignment one day was to take my crew and wash all the windows in the transit barracks, we washed cars the day before. The interesting thing is there was no cleaning gear, just buckets and dirty rags. It was almost impossible to clean a window this way. Moral was in the toilet. Can-Do problem solver DS3 Smith accesses the situation and goes into action 'when you are given command, command'. I threw in a couple dollars of my own money and bought two bottles of Windex at the Mini Navy Exchange store at the end of the barracks complex, the Quad at NAS Alameda. I then organized my guys into teams of sprayers, wipers, inspectors, etc., it was the model of efficiency. Glass in the barracks had never been so clean and in only half a day! The last room to have the windows cleaned was the chief's office. I took my most efficient crew in and like clockwork demonstrated a superior job of military efficiency.

I was immediately reprimanded by the chief, he was yelling at the top of his voice, apparently we were not supposed to get the windows clean, I was to have the crew slave away all day doing 'busy work'...they were not supposed to be done, they were not supposed to be happy, they were not there for teamwork or moral, they were supposed to be miserable, as it should be in a transit barracks. My first lesson in leadership!

The next day I was assigned to the commissary working party, stocking shelves. I never want to do that again. After a couple days I was pulled out and sent to Petty Officer Leadership School where I stayed until the ship returned.

Summer of 67

"Sweet Caroline" – Neil Diamond

Walking in the 'Quad' at NAS Alameda near the transit barracks I happened to meet a very pretty Wave, Carolina Palma. We dated and became fast friends. An actual girlfriend was something I had not had so far in the navy. It seems that anywhere you go the local girls are allergic to sailor suits, don't even try...must be the sailor reputation, undeserved of course.

My high school years were at Waipahu High School in what was then rural Oahu, Hawaii. It was a great place to grow up. I loved everything about it. All the girls I knew were second or third generation Japanese, Korean, Filipino, Chinese, or Polynesian, and a few Caucasians. With that background I was right at home with Carolina who was from the Philippines.

Carolina was very alert and very smart and a great cook. The Waves barracks had a full kitchen, which I never saw because it was off limits. Male visitors had to stay in the lounge area. Carolina would cook dinner and bring it to the lounge and we would dine together. How good is that? They had a pool table too. But no Ping-Pong, oh well.

The USS *Ranger* returns to NAS Alameda

Earlier in the year *Ranger* had come out of a long "yard" period (shipyard overhaul). They had installed all new electronics equipment onboard including all brand new NTDS equipment, my stuff. We were all new and this was a new NTDS ship. In a way it was a blessing, all of us new DS's, right out of school, knew our stuff as we would demonstrate in short order.

Checking in and 'EMI'

I was thrilled to be going aboard that first day. I went around from place to place checking in, OE Division, personnel, medical, bedding and the berthing compartment, sleeping quarters. As soon as I checked in far enough to get my 'Liberty Card' and realized I was not in the duty section, I locked my sea bag to my bunk and left the ship. Had to get back to Carolina, my new girlfriend.

When I arrived back on the ship past midnight I did not know my compartment number, I didn't even know what division I was in! Suddenly it was a very big ship and I had no idea where I was at all. I told the Brow watch I needed to find my compartment. He asked what division I was in... I asked what a division was. It was somewhat embarrassing because I was a 3rd Class petty officer. They asked what I did, and I said I was a Data Systems Technician. That didn't mean anything to them, I said 'electronics' that was still not quite enough. Finally, they called up to the OE Division office, although I was too new to have my name on the record they sent someone down to the hangar deck to escort me. All the ET's and DS's in OE Division slept in 03-231-O-L, a number I should have written down.

By the way, it means "03" third deck above the main deck, Hangar Deck is the main deck, "231" frame 231 aft from the Bow or front of the ship, "O" a compartment that is centered on the centerline of the ship, and "L" which means living quarters.

The compartment number of every compartment in the ship is stamped on a metal tag above every door and large enough to be read with a finger in the event of a smoke-filled room or darkness so dark you don't know if your eyes are open or closed. This information and the complete layout of the ship in your mind are necessary information to save your life. 50 years later I could still find my way around the ship and its 2000 plus compartments blindfolded, I would know exactly where I was in seconds.

But that came with experience. It seems I was having a little trouble getting adjusted to the ship's routine. It could be that staying out past midnight and having trouble getting up in the morning may have had something to do with me ending up with 48 Hrs. EMI (extra military instruction, old fashion military punishment) before I had two weeks on the ship. I now found out what chipping paint and the proper use of a chipping hammer is all about.

Navy electronics schools only prepared me for janitorial duties. I am an artist with a floor buffer not a paintbrush. I learned the navy way.

Reporting aboard as a Third-Class Petty Officer meant that I would not serve in the galley, no mess cooking for me. Normally if you report aboard any ship as a Seaman or Seaman Apprentice you may be sent straight to the galley for six months. PO3 and above would be exempt and go straight to your assigned division.

All the electronics technicians and data systems technicians as well as all this incredible array of radars, communications, computers and digital displays were under OE Division commanded by Lt. Woodward, the EMO.

The navy did an excellent job of installing all this new equipment in *Ranger*. As brand new DS's we were proud to get the chance to be there. It can be the case to be assigned to a ship with older and tired equipment where the volume of routine maintenance dulls the spirit, so to speak. We were lucky.

Where else but the US Navy can you go to a top-notch trade school and then be handed a brand new 50-Million-dollar suite of equipment and told 'go to work it is all yours'. We mostly were all new, only a couple old hands and even they had maybe a year on us. Harry McKee and Ed Buselt are two that come to mind.

Ammo Working Party

Jim Hill PH2

All the bombs and ammunition that were stored in *Ranger* were removed before it went into the shipyard, now they had to be put back. Being a PO3 did not get me above the fray when it came to the "ammunition working party". Unbelievable! Super Carriers like *Ranger* carry more bombs and ammunition than a fleet Ammo ship, more NSFO, naval special fuel oil, than a fleet tanker and more food than an AK supply ship.

Ranger was anchored out in San Francisco Bay for this operation, maybe in case something went wrong. All four deck edge elevators were lowered and loaded barges with cranes from the

Concord Naval Weapons Station were coming and going at each for the next three days. 2000 men working, I was assigned to 500Lb bombs for the first 2 1/2 days. We worked 8 on and 8 off for 24-hour days. On is almost no breaks and no real lunch, 8 off is not much, eat something and crash. It was the most real work I had ever done. We were uncrating 500Lb bombs from their pallets and lifting them onto little yellow carts, two each, and moved the carts over to the bomb elevators where they were taken down to the magazines way below decks. I was beat, after almost three days of 100 plus men in our group working as fast as we could now the 500Lb bombs were all below. With one shift to go we went to help with the 750Lb bombs. These cannot be lifted by four men like the 500's but required a forklift after inserting lifting eyes into the bombs. The entire hangar deck, two football fields, was covered in ordinance of all types' bombs, rockets, missiles, 2000 guys working like crazy. All the 500Lb bomb work was in one small corner of hangar bay 2. I never had to do it again, never lifted another bomb. I still have one of the bomb lifting eyes on my bookshelf as a reminder.

More DS's

Shortly after *Ranger* arrived at NAS Alameda from San Diego and all the transit barracks sailors reported we had quite a crew. We were all learning our positions, making friends and renewing friendships. NTDS specialties were divided into three groups of technicians, Computer, Display and Data Communications. There was one Computer Tech who was onboard that I remembered from Barracks 930 at Mare Island. I didn't know him well then but in *Ranger* in the computer room where we DS's mostly hung out I got to know him. Nice guy, can't remember his name, we had many friendly conversations.

One day while Ranger was still tied up at NAS Alameda a couple guys in suits, never a good sign, came onboard and wanted to question him. Shortly after that he was in the computer room and we were talking privately. He told me that he was being discharged from the navy! I asked him why and he told me frankly that the investigators accused him of being gay and he was being discharged for being gay! I am not sure he was as candid with many of the other guys. Personally I thought of asking him if he was gay but I refrained since it didn't matter to me. I did ask him if he was going to fight it. I was a little surprised when he said he was not. In those days' gays were not allowed to serve and were discharged when it was found that they were gay, no real choice except to make the navy prove it.

Generally I always thought it was a bad thing to be forced out of the military before your obligation was complete and without an Honorable Discharge, guess I still do in a way. As I get older I realize these things depend on circumstances and not all bad. My feeling at the time was that it indicated a job left unfinished.

The rest of the story

Before the ship even left for the first deployment to the Tonkin Gulf in November, he was back visiting onboard *Ranger* but in a civilian suit as a technical representative, 'Tech Rep', for Univac inspecting our computer systems. I was surprised and happy to see him, glad he was doing well and we talked a little. He landed the job with Univac to support NTDS ships, inspecting and generally solving computer problems before the ship sailed. Tech Reps generally did not 'ride' the ships. He was committed to the job, in or out of the navy, I respected him for that.

Men of the World

Two of the ET's I had to work with occasionally were "men of the world" in that they had been in *Ranger* for Cruise 6 and worked through the shipyard period. They thought they knew everything and may have when it came to regular radio comm. gear but knew little of the latest digital synthesized and very sophisticated equipment like the SRC-16. This new equipment could not be repaired with a screwdriver and last year's knowledge, it was far different. We had a few differences of opinion on the maintenance of the SRC-16 but within a short time they were assigned other duties and I had the SRC-16 all to myself.

The "men of the world" were always giving me hell over my girlfriend, soon to be wife, because she was Filipina. They did not respect that at all. More to the story of these two later.

Getting Married, *"Sweet Caroline"* – Neil Diamond

Carolina was born and raised in the Philippines but was a US citizen from birth. I would find out later that Carolina graduated from high school at age 14 and graduated from Philippine Women's University at age 19 as class Valedictorian. Carolina's father, Anastacio, was a US Navy Chief Petty Officer, joined the navy in 1912, participated in the blockade off Vera Cruz Mexico, went into Vera Cruz with the Marines, was in WWI, retired in 1939 in the Philippines. He was recalled to active duty, from the reserves, when the Japanese struck Pearl Harbor and the Philippines, avoided the Bataan Death March and fought with the guerrilla forces on Luzon then retired again in 1947. The family was well off before he collected all his back pay plus combat pay for all of WWII. Anastacio had seven daughters and no sons. In typical CPO fashion he said one of them was going to be in the navy, Carolina was it.

When we met at NAS Alameda Carolina had already been in the navy for almost three years. When I mentioned once wondering if my security clearance would be jeopardized if we married, she simply asked if I knew where the ship was going when it left port, I said

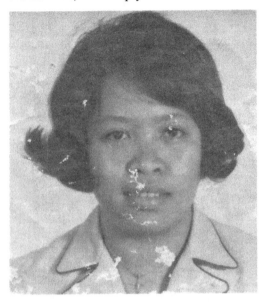

no, we are told when out at sea, she said "I know". End of conversation, Carolina worked in communications at the NAS and her clearance was actually higher than mine at the time. She never told me where the ship was headed, we were both very security conscious.

At that time I did not know that all Waves were either US or Canadian citizens and could pass a security check at some level. The Philippines was a prime recruiting ground for the US Navy since before WWI, for men but not women because of the citizenship requirement. Men joining the US Navy are not required to be US citizens but it will restrict job assignments.

Carolina 1967, Photo, in my wallet for three deployments

Carolina and I got married in our uniforms on Navy Day, 27 October 1967 by a retired commander in Oakland California shortly before *Ranger*'s Cruise 7 started. We didn't know it then but due to conflicting duty assignments we would see each other 45 days total in the next 18 months! It was much better after that, followed by many years of happiness.

At the pool table in the Wave's barracks, a little Spartan but they had curtains and a lamp, nice touch

CHAPTER 7

Going to War

First Deployment, Cruise 7, 1967-1968, 4 November 1967
Captain William T. Donnelly, Jr.

The great summer is over, my first cruise was about to get underway, the Air Wing was aboard and I was excited. The USS *Ranger* was a very impressive ship 'loaded for bear' and ready to go.

USS *Ranger*, CVA-61, morning of departure, 4 November 1967

I had purchased a 1962 Rambler Convertible from my friend Eli Ring for $50 and drove it around from June until November but now we were about to leave. I had not made plans for storage like most who had cars. Carolina was living in the Waves Barracks and she didn't have a driver's license anyway, so what to do with the car? I waited too long to decide and had to go so I drove it to the very large parking lot near the pier and parked in the 'Chief Petty Officers Only' parking, looked around, put the keys in my pocket and sailed away for eight plus months. It was a risk but I figured no one would have the guts to tow a car from the chief's parking lot even if it didn't have the proper sticker on it. Many ships come and go at NAS Alameda, gigantic parking lot, who is to say which cars belong where. Sometimes as many as four aircraft carriers were in port at one time. The car was still there when the ship returned in June 1968, just like a time machine covered in dust. A little fresh gas and a jump, good to go. "Gee the old Rambler ran great, those were the days", as Archie Bunker might say.

Morning of 4 November 1967, moving through San Francisco Bay
The Bay Bridge and Treasure Island in the background

This is Cruise 7 for *Ranger*. In this deployment *Ranger* is the first ship to take the new A7 Corsair II into combat. The squadron was VA-147 'Argonauts'. The US Air Force was evaluating the A7 and some of VA-147 was made up of USAF officers and enlisted. I sat down with two enlisted USAF guys at dinner one evening. I was a 20-year-old PO3 (E4) and one of the AF guys was a balding 32-year-old E5. He was complaining about how he had to 'eat with the troops'. Apparently in the air force E5 was something special. Not so much in *Ranger*.

The Air Force is notorious for being slow to make rank. All us 'Army Brats' knew not to join the air force because of the slow promotions.

USS *Ranger*, CVA-61 passing under the Golden Gate Bridge on the way to the Western Pacific
4 November 1967

ORI in Hawaii

After a week or so at sea, first stop Pearl Harbor. Operational Readiness Inspection. At Pearl Harbor around 600 inspectors boarded *Ranger* and we sailed out to sea for three days of being at war round the clock and testing our reaction to everything from flight operations to CIC operations to fake casualties and crew preparedness for first aid and damage control. Even the method used for cleaning up a broken radioactive electron tube. Everything had to be right or they would not pass us to go into combat.

Apparently we did very well, flying colors you might say. I would say very tired after three days of high stress and almost always at battle stations, combat rations, eating in shifts. What most do not know is when a ship is at general quarters, battle stations, all the hatches are closed and in *Ranger* that means the ship is locked down into two thousand plus small compartments. You need permission from damage control central to even open a hatch (door) to go to the head (restroom). To stay in touch every compartment has a sound powered battle phone to 'Damage Control Central'.

A view of Diamond Head most tourists do not see, Nov 67, our last view of the USA for awhile

---

Visited the old H. S.

After the Tonkin Gulf Incident in 1964 the Vietnam War for the US started to heat up. Waipahu High School was on Farrington highway and right about that time these large double tractor trailer flatbed trucks with covered loads began a constant run from the ammunition magazines (storage) at Kohekohe Pass to the docks in Honolulu. I guessed the war was on. My biggest fear in high school was that the war would be over before I could get there. Seems funny now with seven stars on my Vietnam Service Medal.

I took the bus from Pearl Harbor to Waipahu and visited my old high school. Of course it had only been two and a half years since I was there, class of 65. Had a nice visit with some teachers, talked to a few classes. I was in uniform of course; we were not allowed civilian clothes on the ship. Lots of interest in my job in the navy. As I was standing out in front of the school, sort of one last look, the large double tractor trailer flatbed trucks with covered loads were still roaring by. That's a full three years nonstop. In 1970 when we went into Cambodia we were still dropping the 1943 500 pounders. Didn't get to drop them on Japan, I guess. Unbelievable production during WWII.

Relative Bearing Grease and Wiggy's

When a new seaman apprentice right out of boot camp is assigned to a division it is time for him to get acquainted with the various locations in the ship…right? When an obviously new seaman from the engine room, many decks down, comes into the ET shop on the 03 level, many decks up, inquiring if he is in the right place asking for 'relative bearing grease' we always say that we used to carry that but no more. They have it over at…many decks down and send him on his way there. Of course they know what to do when he gets there. The upside is that you get to know where everything is.

The electricians in *Ranger* often carried an electrical tester referred to as a Wiggy or Wiggins after the manufacturer. This handheld tester resembles a voltmeter except it has no meter, instead it has small neon lamps that indicate standard shipboard voltages from 120 to 440VAC, can also indicate AC or DC and the frequency, 60Hz or 400Hz. A nice easy to use test set.

All hatches and doors on military ships that open to the outside have interlock switches that shut the lights off when the door is opened so that no white light can be seen from the outside at night, white lights at night on a combat ship is a big no-no. It happens that the topmost compartment in *Ranger*, at the top of the island structure, the O-10 level, is a room known as UHF-1 where most of the UHF radio equipment is located. This provides a short cable run to the antennas. UHF-1 has only one door and it opens to the outside, so it has an interlock. The ladder to the door is outside directly across from the SPS-37 radar antenna, a very powerful low frequency radar. It is always rotating when being used and was considered safe as long as it was rotating.

With all this in mind, new electricians were often sent to UHF-1 to troubleshoot a 'complaint' about the door interlock switch not working, "be sure to take your Wiggy". When they got there they found that all the neon lamps on the Wiggy were lit even before it was connected! Pretty scary! Sometimes the new electricians were just dispatched to UHF-1 with an armload of florescent lamps to replace. Of course, climbing up the ladder (stairs) to UHF-1, when the SPS-37 antenna rotates around all the florescent lamps light up right in their hand, another scary moment!

I can't remember what they may have tried on me but I reported aboard *Ranger* as a DS3 so was probably assumed to know this stuff. It is only "fun" when the guy doesn't catch on right away.

There are others but I don't want to reveal all the naval secrets. Anyway they never tire of relative bearing grease, it is still a useful product.

Liberty in Yokosuka

We departed Pearl Harbor, Hawaii headed for Yokosuka, Japan. The stop in Yokosuka was to meet the carrier we were relieving, USS *Constellation*, and exchange certain special weapons across the pier in the dark of night as it were. This operation did not involve very many of the crew, so this was a major first liberty port for almost everyone.

It seems there is always a typhoon between Hawaii and Japan and we sailed into this one as we would one for Cruise 8 and another for Cruise 9. It was rough, I can't say just how rough this one was because I get confused which typhoon was which, rest assured they were all rough. Essentially it is like being on the biggest, meanest, rollercoaster for about four to five days non-stop. More than 50% of the crew is seasick. I made it through by keeping my stomach full of saltine crackers. Stop eating and get sick! As the old saying goes about being seasick, "first you are afraid you are going to die, then you are afraid you aren't". I never got seasick on *Ranger* but did on a 75' sailboat out of Monterey Bay 20 years later.

Yokosuka Japan November 1967

ET Master Chief Joyner was not only our Master Chief in OE Division and later 'Chief of the Boat', he was a chief before I was born so we all cut him some slack. Chief Joyner called all the 'new' guys, men who had not been overseas before, into the ET Shop 2 for a little indoctrination speech. Went something like this, "I know many of you guys are going to go exploring the various bars and other places, possibly of ill repute. When you are sitting there drinking with some young lady I want you to carefully count your drinks, each time you pick up the drink to take a sip keep in mind 'this is my second, etc.'. If you pick up a drink and you can't remember if it is the fourth or the fifth then set it back down and return to the ship while you still have your money". Sounds like very reasonable advice for a young sailor.

The party

Of course, Svenson and I were not going to cruise any bars, we were going to tour around, see the sights and checkout a few shops. As it turns out OE Division was organizing a grand party, it seems we had some professional party organizers in OE Div. The party was scheduled for 6PM and everyone planned to be there, bring your girl if you found one, several did. OE Division had around 100 men add to that the special guests like the Chaplin and some Officers, it was a big party. Svenson and I arrived on time, things were underway, a lot of fun. It was an open bar. I had never drunk hard liquor before and when they ask me what I wanted I didn't know what to say. The guy in front of me asked for a 'seven and seven', that sounded good so I got one too.

The drinks went down fast, after six or seven, maybe more, I suddenly couldn't count my fingers much less the drinks. So much for the chief's advice. The party was just getting started good. DS1 Newhard put a goldfish in his beer and drank it down on a bet. Part of the entertainment was this very pretty, as I recall, Japanese dancer on the small stage, I took another drink. She was a stripper as it turns out, I really don't remember anything else about the party. The next thing I knew I was in a Taxi arriving at the ship with my jumper and Pea coat across my arm. I couldn't figure out why I didn't have some of my clothes on. Anyway no time to dwell on that, I spent the rest of the night "calling for Ralph" in the head. I never felt so bad.

Back out at sea the guys were all telling stories of how I was up on stage and taking off as much as she was taking off, I thought they were telling sea stories just to get at me. Usual shipboard harassment of new guys. In those days when you took photos you had to send the roll of film in to be developed. A couple weeks later the photos started coming in. They were posted in ET Shop 2; I took them down and tossed them as soon as the amusement wore off. Guess it wasn't a sea story after all. Should have saved them, we could all laugh now. I had no idea I would write a book 50 years later.

Me and Harry McKee and Annabelle, computer #1
Greg Boyd's new Sony tape deck in the background will play music continuously for the next three years

On-Line, Tonkin Gulf

We arrived on-line in the Tonkin Gulf in early December and started combat operations right away. I was excited by all the activity. First time in the war for me, even though I was in the ship and not in a fox hole. I was in awe of the pilots...they were going in harm's way every day. Busy day on the flight deck.

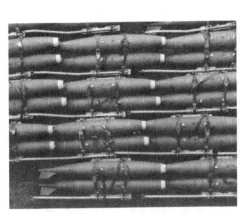

Looking down on 500-pound bombs
waiting on the
starboard side of the island

Loading 500-pound bombs on an A6 Intruder

Bombs loaded, time to insert the fuzzes

Safety first, attaching the safety wires
they will be removed just before launch

A7 Corsair II from VA-147 Argonauts

A6A Intruders from VA-165, Boomers on the waist CATs

Cut em' loose

F4 on the CAT ready to launch

Afterburners visible, VF-154 Black Knights, Phantom launches off the waist CAT
while A4C's from VA-22, Fighting Redcocks, move to the forward CATs

A7 launches from the waist CAT, A4C's moving to the forward CATs

TV Transmitter, Bob Hope Show
and
Raquel Welch

The Bob Hope show was scheduled to perform aboard *Ranger* on 21 December, I was called into the EMO office and told I would be temporarily assigned to KRAN, the ships TV station for the duration of the Bob hope show. Sounds OK but it was extra duty, oh well. Anyway no choice. The first thing I was assigned to was repairing the ships TV transmitter. It was little more than a homemade transmitter, a piece of work, I felt like I could do better building one from scratch. I worked with ET Chief Shope on it and we got it working. KRAN was a closed-circuit TV station for the crew. It had TV monitors in most compartments and other rooms where the crew gathered, it did not transmit over the air. In this case they wanted to transmit to the other ships that would be close by.

Bob Hope with les Brown in the background

It was a lucky break after all, when the Bob Hope entourage came aboard I was assigned to escort Les Brown around the ship and to chow. He wanted to eat with the crew and not in the officers' wardroom. He didn't even want to go to the head of the line so we waited in line and talked to everyone that came by.

But best of all just before the big show was going to start on the flight deck and things were getting organized I was assigned to sit in the little KRAN studio with Raquel Welch and keep her company. Just the two of us. As I am sitting there with her and chatting small talk, very nice conversation with a real movie star, I kept thinking shouldn't there be a Marine here guarding Raquel. A very nice person, the real deal. After about 15 minutes someone came in and said, 'time to go up on deck'. The KRAN studio was just below the fight deck 03 starboard just a little forward of the island. Any women visiting the ship at sea were usually accompanied by a Marine…as if they didn't trust a sailor.

I had a very good position for the show, took a lot of photos and was hoping I would not run out of film. When I got to 36 (slide film) then 37, 38 my heart sank. The film was not loaded properly and had not advanced, rats! Raquel did give me an autographed official photo but it was lost in time. Now that I think about it, I never did get to meet Bob Hope in person. Les Brown and Raquel Welch was as close as I got but that was just great.

Raquel Welch performing with Les Brown and his Band of Renown
USS *Ranger*, 21 December 1967

Christmas 1967
Online Yankee Station

Didn't take any photos of the little tree we had set up in the computer room. This would be the first of three Christmas' in a row on Yankee Station, away from my new wife. We listened to a few songs, OK back to work. Many times our 'work' consisted of waiting for something to break so we could work on it.

Carolina sent me some fruitcakes that were absolutely soaked in Rum and sealed nicely. Suddenly I had friends that loved fruitcake. The Rum fruitcakes became an annual Christmas treat every Christmas I was in *Ranger*.

Carolina was a masterful cook, later in life she would become fluent in French and study at Le Cordon Bleu in Paris to become a pastry chef. She apprenticed at the 'Top of the Mark', Mark Hopkins in San Francisco.

Electronics, the TGC Module

The four transmitters in the SRC-16 Communications Central equipment sometimes suffered from the power output either being too low or too high or not responding properly. I discovered the problem was the TGC module or Transmit Gain Control, this module had a chopper stabilized servo amplifier that operated a small motor driven potentiometer to control the gain of the transmitter. The servo amplifier was four

subminiature tubes that were soldered in. This is not something that you normally repair on the ship, just get another module from supply. However, the ones in supply had the same problem so I ordered tubes and motor driven potentiometers and took each one apart and soldered in the new components. I had the best operating SRC-16 in the fleet after that. Later Lt. Woodward had me document what I did and it was sent to the fleet. I also rewrote the AN/SRC-16 PMS, Preventative Maintenance Schedule, cards that described the various procedures for preventative maintenance. These were submitted and accepted fleet wide. I was surprised that someone was listening after all. The original cards were produced by Collins Radio and did not reflect the experience we had in the fleet with the equipment. Good job Smith, why are you still standing here, get back to work.

New Year 1968

New Year's 1968 Celebration in Subic Bay and Olongapo City

We spent Christmas at sea on Yankee Station but in exchange we got to spend the New Year's celebration in Subic. My first assignment to Shore Patrol duty, new guy, guess what, you have Shore Patrol. I didn't mind the duty and routinely exchanged the duty with some of the others so when we went to Hong Kong and back to the US, I didn't have shore patrol at all. The celebration for the New Year was a wild time in Olongapo City.

Making a tape home, Radar Switchboard Room, my new Norelco Carrycorder 150

'Men of the World', Karma Catches Up

At the *Ranger* reunion in June 2009 I met several ET's and DS's from OE Division, Cruise 7 and was trying to place everyone, older now. As we were all telling sea stories I suddenly realized who one guy was, it was one of the "Men of the World" as I choose to call them. The two guys who always gave me hell and made unruly comments about my Filipina wife. The light came on, I said something to the effect of 'I have a great story'. He looked at me and knew and shook his head very slightly as if to say 'please don't'. So I didn't tell. I will tell now but not use the names because I promised not to. I suspect he remembered me first and was waiting for me to recognize him. As things like this go he is a very nice guy and we were all young once. I always thought you can laugh about things that are 10 years or more in the past but maybe some are still embarrassing.

Generally I didn't drink or smoke and because I was married I was not a candidate for the usual sailor bar hopping in Olongapo City when the ship was in Subic. Instead I often volunteered to exchange Shore Patrol duty with others. Each ship is required to supply some number of Petty Officers on a rotating assignment for Shore Patrol duty in each port. When a ship like *Ranger* docks with 4500 to 5000 men it is necessary to reinforce the local Shore Patrol (Military Police). As a result over my many times in Olongapo I was probably in more bars than any dedicated bar hopper.

So one day, could have been when *Ranger* was in Subic for New Year 1968, was right around this time, early Cruise 7, I was on duty at the shore patrol main station just inside the gate. At that time many restrictions were in place, 'Cinderella Liberty', meaning you had to be back across the bridge on US Navy soil by midnight. Another was you had to stay on the main street, miles of bars anyway, meaning side alleys or visiting anyplace not on the main drag was strictly Off-Limits unless you were on official business.

Of course, being men of the world, those rules were for regular sailors not for experienced men of the world. So, as the story goes, the two unnamed individuals were down an alley in a building gambling with several Filipinos when something went wrong. I don't know if they were losing and didn't want to pay or were winning and wanted to leave. In any event there was a scuffle and they reportedly exited the building through a window and were seen running down the alley with several Filipino men with knives in hot pursuit. They ran into a blind alley with a three or four-foot wall at the end and easily leaped over it and strait into an open sewer! Both of them standing chest deep in sewage right about the pockets on a tropical dress white uniform shirt. The Filipinos were reportedly laughing so hard they decided not to kill them. Why would I know all this, sea story you say? No, poetic justice, I was there to hose them off outside when the Hard Hats, permanent Shore Patrol, brought them into the shore patrol main station! OK boys, clothes off! Both left wrapped in navy blankets in a van headed for *Ranger* at Cubi Point seven miles from the main gate at Subic. I did not say anything back in the ship but they apparently told some others and word got around about the incident.

The upside is they never said another ill word to me. They were both routinely transferred from *Ranger* after the cruise for reasons not having to do with any incident.

At the AN/SPA-8 old fashion Radar Repeater we use to check Radar video

Pueblo Incident

Toward the end of January 1968 *Ranger* was completing about 19 days on Yankee Station, about the normal online period in the combat zone. Flags and other regalia were being put up in the hangar bay preparing for a ceremony of some sort that would be attended by many high-ranking officials from South Vietnam. I do not know exactly what the ceremony was about but it was just before TET, maybe that was part of it.

Suddenly there was a great amount of activity in the combat information center (CIC), word was the Captain received an eyes-only message, no one knew what it was about. The date was 23 January. The USS Pueblo had been boarded and seized on the high seas by North Korea. Suspiciously just in time to distract from the upcoming TET offensive by North Vietnam.

I guessed the party was off when Captain Donnelly came on the 1MC to talk to the crew. Paraphrasing he said that we were needed elsewhere, that the Carrier Division 3 Admiral and his staff would be transferred off the *Ranger* as quickly as possible, that NO communications were to leave the ship from this second on, swift punishment for anyone even slipping a letter or note to anyone being transferred off. On the NTDS consoles we could see our escorts heading north at high speed. It took, as I recall, maybe two hours plus to get everyone off. The Admiral has a contingent of about 250 persons which included his band, they had to hustle. The helicopters were coming from everywhere.

We sped off north and within hours caught up with our escorts. We were later to learn the USS *Pueblo* was captured by North Korea just outside the NK territorial limit.

The weather was getting colder as we progressed north but things were heating up on the rumor mill. On the way north word came down to reconfigure all the A4C Skyhawks to 'single weapon carrier', well there is only one weapon that is worth carrying just one of! And the A4 was known to be good at delivering it.

We arrived in the Yellow Sea off South Korea and variously operated in the area of the Yellow Sea, East China Sea and the Sea of Japan. One day the word in CIC was 'a lot of ships out there', I went out to look around, took my camera. Four Carriers, Heavy Cruisers, Destroyers, supply ships, ships everywhere, looked like a WWII invasion.

USS *Enterprise*, CVAN-65 ahead of us, departing from the supply ship, we're next
other ships waiting for the starboard side of the supply ship
Note the unmistakable island structure of *Enterprise*

Right after topping off in the Yellow Sea the *Enterprise* and *Ranger* headed into a heavy fog and went to Condition EMCON A, no radio or radar emissions, in other words we became invisible, and no escorts. We headed for the Tsushima Straight, the Russian 'Trawlers' that were hounding us could not keep up. They had to know we were making a run for the Sea of Japan so they positioned a 'Trawler' in the middle of the Tsushima Straight and one in the middle of the Korea Straight. It was something to behold, two giant CVA's hugging the coast of Japan blacked out and using fathometers to navigate. I went out on the flight deck to see and thought maybe I could hit a baseball into Japan, seemed that close at night, the mountains of Japan helped hide our silhouette. Our ECM was working well that day, middle of the night we could see the masthead lights on the Trawler and they could not see us on their radar, wow! Of course we could see everything on our scopes in CIC because the NTDS data communication was receiving all the track information from other NTDS ships all over the Sea of Japan and Yellow Sea. We didn't need our Radar to know where everybody was.

USS *Coral Sea* waiting behind us, Choppy Seas off Korea
notice guys working on the aircraft…it is cold out there

Heavy Cruiser USS *Saint Paul* nearby *Ranger* in the Yellow Sea

Now *Ranger*, CVA-61 and the *Enterprise*, CVAN-65 were operating in secret in the middle of the Sea of Japan. It was known that some reconnaissance was taking place by the Russians, the North Koreans would not venture out. No one was coming close to us; we could see everything on NTDS without using our radars and revealing where we were.

While we were hiding out in the Sea of Japan the fleet was looking for 17 North Korean submarines. Old diesel boats but could be dangerous. The ASW effort was very large. Word was that over 200 sub-surface contacts were detected in the Sea of Japan and general operating area. We had ASW assets parked over all of them. I am sure many were our own but you can't tell whose it is when it is underwater. In full combat mode a sonic, ping if you will, message is sent by sonar and bounces off the hull for all in the submarine to hear. An international message that essentially means 'active combat zone, surface and identify or be sunk'. If they don't come up a homing torpedo goes in the water and it is not like in the movies, it is goodbye submarine.

Routinely in CIC the display consoles were showing Migs over North Korea taking off from an airstrip inland and being 'locked on' immediately by US Navy ships. The Talos missiles carried by guided missile cruisers have a range of over 100 miles. N. Korea is small, and we had them 'locked on' before they got their wheels folded. A Guided Missile Cruiser and DLG (guided missile destroyer, Terrier Missiles) were cruising up and down the coast of N. Korea locking missiles on everything that moved. In the Migs, as in our aircraft, they have a radio receiver that warns them if a fire control radar is locked on the aircraft, they were probably getting that beep as the wheels came up.

An A3 Whale setting up on the waist CAT, wings still folded
choppy water of the Yellow Sea off South Korea

Some South Korean military officers came onboard *Ranger* earlier, I am sure for co-ordination purposes. My first time to see high ranking South Korean Officers.

Finally came the day and we all got a look at the big show. From CIC we could see the entire task force went to 'General Quarters', battle stations. On the *Ranger* flight deck half the aircraft were armed for a conventional strike, regular bombs, etc., and half with nuclear weapons. The marines were everywhere, no photos allowed. There never is when the 'special' ordinance is being handled. Can't even tell you what color they are, rumored to be black. Rumor was the *Enterprise* had a full nuclear strike ready. I was trying to think of how to describe this...it was probably the usual contingency planning as the entire US Military was on alert. I had unfettered access to CIC but not to mission planning. I had no idea about plans, just watching the action. CIC was real time command and control at the tactical level, no information about where planes go or their targets. Target planning is IOIC land.

The US Strategic Weapons indicator in CIC went to 'Yellow', this usually means 'no drill, B-52's in the air, uncover the Minuteman missiles. I read several books about the Pueblo Incident to see if anyone mentioned any of this, can't find it. Task force weapons indicator went to 'Red', means every ship at battle stations, no drill, weapons ready.

In CIC, besides all the usual activity of tracking and assigning weapon systems to various targets, two destroyers loaded with Combat Marines were approaching Wonsan Harbor on the N. Korean east coast where the USS *Pueblo* was docked. Things started to heat up as the two destroyers approached the 10-mile territorial limit then, suddenly, it was canceled. All I know. I am guessing they found out the crew had already been taken elsewhere in N. Korea and towing out an empty ship under fire would not be a great idea. However that information was way 'above my pay grade' as they say.

A day or so later *Ranger* and *Enterprise* were discovered by a Japanese private plane carrying a news reporter. I learned later that it was big news, photos and all "*Ranger* Found". There is always a lot you don't know about what is going on at home or in the newspapers when you are one person in the ship.

SRC-16 Control Panel   SRC-16 Transmitter #1 pulled out for maintenance

USS *Yorktown*

The USS *Yorktown* (CVS-10) and their TV transmitter

The USS *Yorktown* had a very nice TV station donated to the ship, transmitter, mixing panels, video tape and all. Lt Woodward wanted me to fly over and look at it. Our TV station was OK but our TV transmitter was very homemade. ET Chief Shope and I barely got it working before the Bob Hope show. Lt. Woodward wanted to see if we could up our game. The *Yorktown* was busy with ASW, anti-submarine warfare, work during the Pueblo Incident but I managed to fly over when it was close by to see their system.

Approaching USS *Yorktown* CVS-10

Part of the TV Transmitter in *Yorktown*

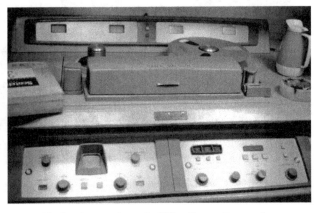

Notice the very latest in Video Tape…Impressive

It was nice as can be seen in the photos, all donated. I stayed aboard the day and was happy to get back to the *Ranger*, things were happening. When I returned to the *Ranger* they were at General Quarters (battle stations), thankfully it was just a drill.

Sasebo

We made a port of call in Sasebo Japan after 63 days at sea. At the time one of the longest at sea periods for any ship since WWII and Korea.

Liberty in Sasebo was great. I went on a bus tour to see the sights; I usually didn't bother with sightseeing tours in general. I preferred shopping for Hi-Fi gear. It was interesting, there was a pretty young stewardess onboard who sang a lot of songs and entertained. Apparently, they entertain on tour buses as a way to get recognized in the entertainment and movie industry. Everyone was well behaved, not the usual bus load of sailors. The bus stopped at a little store; a soda stand type place by the side of the road. Everyone got off the bus, just then a group of Japanese students, maybe 12 years old or so, were walking by in their very uniform uniforms with backpacks to match. Looked nice so we all got out our new Yashica Electro-35 cameras and started taking photos, then the children stopped and dug into their backpacks and started taking photos of us with their Nikon SLR cameras. I got back on the bus.

Hong Kong 1968

It was my first time to visit Hong Kong. It was still British but very rustic, that is to say very Asian. I had no shore patrol and went shopping every day I didn't have duty. I didn't buy much but a lot of looking.

One thing about Hong Kong was the food, it was fabulous. Once I even took the ferry over just to go to a fancy restaurant and have a crabmeat cocktail, great. In one case ten of us went into a nice restaurant, we were very welcome. Talk about service, there were five waiters standing by just at our table for the ten of us. Wine glasses remained full.

Ranger anchored out in the bay. The ship looked pretty tired after so many months at sea. When US Navy ships visit Hong Kong harbor there is a rule that no maintenance of combat arms can be done. So we could not work on the equipment at all. The aircraft were all arranged on the flight deck. The hangar deck was full of Chinese laundry vendors and other vendors that were qualified to be invited aboard. Of course each was watched closely, no leaving the business stall. I got all my laundry done right.

These boys would jump into the water and retrive coins thrown in the water by the sailors waiting for the ferry boat to depart

View of Hong Kong, May 1968

Another view of Hong Kong, May 1968

Back to the Tonkin Gulf and the War, Lots of time online

Finally after more 'line periods' on Yankee Station it was time to go home. We left for Yokosuka Japan, now as the relieved Carrier. The Captain gave permission to purchase motorcycles and bring them onboard to be stored on the hangar deck with the proviso that if we were called back to combat the motorcycles were going over the side!

Being recalled when on the way home is something that is not common. But it had happened to another carrier recently due to the Pueblo incident.

A roll of the dice but happy to report we were not recalled to combat and all the motorcycles made it to Alameda safely. Not sure how many lasted long after that. Happy sailors all.

Just trapped an RA5C Vigilante, USS *Kitty Hawk* (CVA-63) and her Plane Guard in the background

Blast shields up, busy day at the office for the pilots

Jim Hill PH2

Argonauts VA-147 A7's over USS *Ranger* CVA-61

Jim Hill PH2

RA5C Vigilante
trapping aboard
'Plane Guard'
destroyer in
position behind
Ranger

VA-147, A7 Corsair II trapping aboard Ranger

CHAPTER 9

Returning Home to NAS Alameda June 1968

If you are going to San Francisco – Scott McKenzie

Seems like that song was the *Ranger* theme song. It was a grand homecoming. Carolina was there to meet me. More than a thousand people met the ship. Everyone was excited.

Sailors are a superstitious lot. For example, many of the guys bought Timex watches to wear during the cruise...and tossed them overboard when we returned back in under the Golden Gate Bridge. I was wearing the watch my parents gave me in high school and I declined to toss it in the water. I guess enough watches went in the water the karma covered me too.

My car was still there in the chief's parking lot. Just dusted it off, mixed in a little fresh gas and a jump. Good to go.

I guess Carolina and I seemed like the original DINK's (Dual Income No Kids). I was now a DS2 and Carolina was still in the navy but about to get out at NAS Alameda. While I was away Carolina rented a small apartment at the Bayview Apartments at 470 Central Ave. just outside the base in Alameda. We even went to Whitefront in Oakland and bought a new 12" black and white TV including a rinky-dink stand! We bought a new couch too...and had it delivered, that will keep the neighbors talking!

Discovered a new program on TV, 'Star Trek', very cool. I would have to see most of it years later on reruns.

RAV in Bremerton

There was no opening at Hunters Point Naval Shipyard across San Francisco Bay from Alameda, our homeport, to have the necessary maintenance performed on *Ranger* to get her ready for the next deployment in November. It takes three months of a 'short' yard period, referred to as an RAV (Restricted Availability) to make all repairs and get the ship up to date including a new paint job.

The navy decided to 'temporally' change the home port of *Ranger* to the Puget Sound Naval Shipyard in Bremerton Washington. I was disappointed at this turn of events as Carolina was still in the navy at NAS Alameda and I would not get to see her before the next cruise started except on a short leave.

Cars on the Ranger flight deck being transported to Bremerton, I left the Rambler in Alameda

Because of the temporary change of homeport the navy agreed to take families, cars, campers, etc. to Bremerton in the ship. Half of the flight deck was covered with cars. Lots of folks riding up in the ship.

On the way to Bremerton off the coast of California just for fun there was a plan to launch an old car off the ship using the forward port catapult (Cat). These catapults are steam driven and can easily take a 26-ton aircraft from stop to 220mph in 1/25th of a mile, the length of the Cat. They had a big ceremony to launch this old car. The shoe of the Cat was tied to the front bumper but it just pulled the bumper off and tossed it out to sea. The car was then secured a little better but not good enough for lots of power from the Cat so it just sort of rolled off the front of the ship, not very impressive, many 'boos'.

They got serious next and brought out a steel net, laid it out and rolled another car into it, folded over the top like a bag and hooked it to the Cat. The Air Boss comes running out shouting that it was his car, "what is going on"! I think it was part of the show. The Captain promised him a new 'beater' just as good as that one and the show went on. With the car secured in the steel net they apparently decided to really put the poop to the Cat, maybe because of all the 'boos' from the first try. In any event the second try was impressive. The car collapsed a little inside the net as the Cat accelerated. The acceleration was so great parts were flying off the car, door handles, etc. as it went the 1/25th of a mile on the ship and then about another good half mile or more out to sea. Who says old cars can't fly! Great show. Talk about being at the 'Drag races'! Well over 200Mph in 211 feet!

Protecting ourselues from the latest Russian Missiles

It was well known that North Vietnam had the Russian STYX missile and they put them on motor torpedo boats and tried to get close enough to American ships to fire them.

The STYX missile uses radar to guide it to the target. Technically it uses a 'conical scan' radar. That is one that scans in a circle in front of it as it closes in on the target, much like you might do with a flashlight in the woods at night, circling the light in front so you can see everything. The radar looks for changes in the movement of the target and makes corrections based on a change of direction in a 360-degree conical search area in front of the missile.

The AN/ULQ-6 was a countermeasures equipment in *Ranger* during this time. I know it is OK to talk about it because things are much more sophisticated now, and besides, I saw one in an electronics surplus junk yard 15 years ago. The ULQ-6 would receive the radar signal from the STYX that was seeking us and tune up a transmitter on the same frequency then, depending on the mode selected, it would gradually adjust power and substitute its own transmitted signal to fake out the normal radar echo to the missile. All this happening in milliseconds. Now the missile thinks it has a strong echo but it is actually being faked out, it can no longer see its own echo. The ULQ-6 can then, with a simple phase shift of the transmitted echo, cause the missile to either 'walk off' the target and splash or it can make the destroyer behind us look like an aircraft carrier and us look like a destroyer or lose its track altogether. There were a couple other modes but since I didn't really work on that equipment I don't know them all. It is ET stuff.

When the STYX missile got close to the target it would put its radar into a high-power mode, using the remaining battery power to have one last look around but by that time there was nothing to look at. That was the plan anyway. This is known as 'Burn Thru' mode.

During the 67-68 cruise it was believed that North Vietnamese motor torpedo boats that got close could launch these missiles in 'Burn Thru' mode and the couple watts power of the ULQ-6 would not be strong enough to deal with the powerful echo of a missile in 'Burn Thru' mode.

In practice we never let them get close enough to actually launch a missile but we needed to be protected.

During the RAV yard period at Bremerton, WA in the summer of 1968 two entire rooms were welded to the sides of the ship on the 03-level outboard of the flight deck, one port and one starboard. Each room contained a 5kW Traveling Wave Tube or TWT amplifier for the respective ULQ-6 transmitter. More than enough power to fake out the strongest radar on a missile even if it is in 'Burn Thru' mode.

Advanced Firefighting School:

The USS *Forrestal* CVA-59 was online in the Tonkin Gulf on July 29, 1967. Their first air strike of the day was arranged on the flight deck, all the planes were loaded with bombs and rockets. The aircraft are arranged (spotted) in a "U" shape formation on the after part of the flight deck so they can be pulled out and launched from one of four catapults. The carrier was turned into the wind and had the necessary 30 knots of wind down the flight deck. The first aircraft were on the 'Cats' when a rocket from one of the waiting planes accidentally launched from the port side and hit an aircraft on the starboard side of the "U". There was fire and explosions from all sides that ended with 134 dead and 161 injured.

In that incident many of the first crew causalities were the Damage Control personnel, the professional firefighters. They were fighting fires when bombs blew up in front of them. Every sailor has some firefighting training, so help was not a problem. The problem was leadership, not enough well-trained leaders to lead the men into fires "where Angels fear to tread" so to speak, especially that day.

As a result the navy decided that all senior petty officers on aircraft carriers would go through a special advanced firefighting school that concentrated on leading sailors in firefighting. Leadership was what they were after. Of course it is necessary to know what you are doing too.

Of course, "Smith, you are in the first wave". It was a very intensive school. I knew this was not going to be the easy boot camp firefighting thing all over again when I noticed they had ambulances standing by every day. The school was five long and tiring event filled days. Every day started with each hose team standing by their equipment for inspection, after inspection the instructor blew a whistle and all ten teams, five teams facing five teams, assembled their hoses as quickly as possible and began hosing down the other groups. The stream of water from a 2 1/2-inch fire hose will knock you right off your feet, oh, and you will be wet too. Start the day miserable, get used to it.

There were classes on all types of shipboard firefighting, equipment, methods, chemicals, PKP (Purple K Powder) for fuel fires, CO_2 for electrical fires, water, foam, etc.

At Puget Sound the navy had a ship the size of a small destroyer up on dry land. In many drills we were down several decks in full Oxygen Breathing Apparatus, (OBA) with hoses putting out fires in the engine room and other spaces. Someone got hurt every day I was there. They were very serious about this training.

You are supposed to aim the water stream at the base of the fire. In one exercise we had three teams approaching the engine room from different directions where there was a fire at one end of the room. The guy on the nozzle for team 1, I was number 2 on team 2, pulled the stream high and the fire flashed back fast under the engine room deck. The chief instructor was only saved by the 'fog' team. I guess all part of the plan. Remember "The Sea stalks the unwary and relentlessly pursues the careless".

Over the next two cruises in *Ranger* I only donned an OBA once for real. I taught the class several times. Starting a cruise just before arriving at Pearl Harbor we had a fire forward on the 03 level. Some work uniforms were stowed improperly in a Void. This Void was not suitable to store anything because it had a superheated steam pipe running through it to the forward catapults but the pipe was not marked as it should have been. In port when the uniforms were stowed there was no steam in the pipes and all looked OK. At sea the uniforms smoldered and caught fire, blew a bolted hatch off and ripped 1/4-inch steel like paper. The ship went to General Quarters, about fifteen minutes into the fire I was told to assemble my fire team and don OBA's but not to charge the cartridges until we were needed. Rumor was they carried a couple guys out of the fire area on stretchers, this was news enough to cause one of my guys to be really scared to the point that he was crying and could not put on his OBA, slid down the bulkhead (wall) and sat on the deck. I was yelling at him to get up and finally booted him a little, he got mad and stood up, then I told him to put on the OBA. He was OK after that. Within about 45 minutes or so of all this a Damage Control Chief came by and said we could stand down. Everything was under control; we would not be needed after all.

Every Sailor buys a New Car

Carolina and I took three weeks leave and went to Michigan where Dad was the Army recruiter. This was part of the 45 days Carolina and I had together in our first 18 months of marriage. Carolina and I also visited my grandparents and other relatives in Lock Haven Pennsylvania, it was a great time. Lock Haven is an old town and in the summer of 1968 there were very few to no people in the town that were anything but white. I think most people had never been out of Clinton County. Maybe they saw an Asian on TV, even TV was limited to a couple channels, but never saw a person from the Philippines. Carolina and I walked into the bank in town and all transactions stopped cold! We knew we weren't in California anymore. Everyone we met treated Carolina very well. I think at the time most people in Lock Haven did not know what racism was, that is something you have to be taught I guess.

Had a great time visiting the family in Michigan as well. In Michigan, Carolina and I bought a brand new 1968VW 'Bug'. We loaded it with the few possessions mom and dad had stored in the basement for me.

Our brand new 1968 VW Bug

Pack it like a sea bag, next stop Bremerton, WA

Carolina with Gram and Pop during our visit to Pennsylvania

We had a great time driving the new bug cross country to Bremerton, WA The northern route just looked easier from Michigan but at one point I started to wonder after driving across North Dakota for more than two hours at 65mph and seeing no cars at all, not even coming the other way! No points of reference either. Back then before GPS it was all about maps and points of reference …like a city or even a town, OK, give me a side road that is on the map! Just keep going west young man.

After checking in on *Ranger* we drove to Alameda and I took a plane back to Bremerton.

My Grandfather

In 1917 my grandfather, Frank A. Swinehart, was the only one of twelve brothers to go to France to fight in WWI. 'Pop', as part of the 314th Regiment, 79 Division, fought in intensive combat at the battle of the Meuse Argonne in WWI. Pop was well known in the community as a local hero and as a person always ready to help others. Pop could always be seen wearing his WWI 'Campaign Hat', replaced many times over the years as they wore out.

Pop taught all the grandchildren to shoot from an early age. Later, as we went into the military, he spent more time with Jerry and I because he thought we may be in combat.

FRANK A. SWINEHART
Corpral, Co. A, 314th Infantry,
79th Division, U. S. Army, 1917
Camp Meade, Maryland

Army Warrant Officer

Back at Alameda, Army Warrant, almost a soldier

When I made E-5 (DS2) I decided to apply for army warrant officer, known as 'cross decking' to the army. The rule was to apply for army warrant, W-1, you had to be an E-5, to apply for navy warrant you had to be E-6 so I thought I would try the army first. I often thought of being a helicopter pilot but I knew that was out because of my vision, I would have to leave that one to my brother Jerry, 3 years younger than me and my son Ron, 38 years later. I looked at the list of possibilities and decided to apply for the 'HAWK' anti-aircraft guided missile system. It was somewhat close to what I was doing in the navy in terms of command and control systems. I felt I could make a significant contribution to the army in that capacity. I submitted the proper paperwork to the army directly without going through any official channels on the ship.

To my amazement I was called for an interview at the US Army Headquarters at the Presidio in San Francisco. I reported in my best uniform and was interviewed by a panel of five officers. I thought it went well enough. They said the army would get back to me. They did. One day Lt. Woodward called me into the EMO office and handed me the response, well I guess the secret was out, the army sent it to the *Ranger*. The letter said I was accepted for appointment but quoted out for a billet, "please reapply in six months". I read that as we want you but no open position at this time.

Much later as an E-6 I applied for navy warrant officer, many PO1's apply for warrant officer because it was a good way to get a look at the chief's test. You have to be in the navy eight years before you can even apply to go up for chief. I was a long way from that but there was no waiting period for warrant officer.

By the time the navy processed the application I was three months out of the navy and working in a truly great position as a field engineer for Digital Equipment Corporation, the second largest computer company in the US. The letter wanted to know if I would like to come back into the navy and accept my appointment to W-1. I knew that a W-1 appointment in the navy is a temporary assignment, if you fail to be promoted to W-2 in one year you revert to your former enlisted rank. That is why all navy W-1's are the greatest 'boot lickers' ever and I was sure my hard charging attitude would land me back as an E-6 so I declined. Later I found out that all on my list, I had two friends on the list, went directly to Lt JG (O2) as LDO's (Limited Duty Officer), for example Electronics Officer. If I knew that I might have gone back. You just never know, the navy does that sometimes.

CHAPTER 10

Second Deployment

Second Deployment, Cruise 8, 1968–1969, 26 October 1968
Captain W.H. Livingston

Left on my second deployment with Carolina in a new apartment, The Lincoln House at 2235 Lincoln Ave. in Alameda, and our new car, we gave the old Rambler to one of Carolina's friends. Carolina had finished her four years in the navy and took a job as a chemist at the Coca Cola bottling plant in Oakland. By the time I got back she changed jobs and was working in one of the offices at NARF (Naval Air Rework Facility) at NAS Alameda.

ORI in Hawaii, the usual, we did well and were on our way, another typhoon, Sven and I didn't get sick again but so many others did. The chow lines are shorter in bad weather. Stopped again in Yokosuka, Japan. No party this time. Lesson learned.

Back to the Tonkin Gulf Yacht Club, now a DS2

Secret Squirrels

When we made the port of call in Yokosuka, the usual stop on the way to the war, it was cold so the 'Uniform of the Day' was blues. There is an order when leaving the ship. The officers have their own walkway known as the 'Officers Brow' and the enlisted have the 'After Brow', of course this is when the ship is docked to a pier.

The departing order is Chief Petty Officers first, then First Class Petty Officers and so on. I was a second class and I knew all the Electronics Technicians by sight and by name. So I am standing with the second classes waiting to depart the ship and the guy next to me is wearing a Pea Coat with an ET-2 rating patch on his sleeve. I figured he stole or borrowed the coat so he could get off sooner, this has been known to happen. I quietly asked him if he was an ET and he said yes. I just knew that was a lie so I asked what division he was in and he said OE. I knew that was a lie too. I told him he should come with me and prove it, he did, and we went to the EMO Office. Mr. Woodward was there and I asked him if this guy was really an ET and he said yes. I apologized to him and he left. Then Mr. Woodward told me he was actually a CT. They are ET's that get assigned this special duty out of ET school much like DS's but wear the ET insignia. It turns out that he was part of the group no one knows about, secret intercept operators, listening to enemy radio messages, etc. I suddenly remembered that in port at Alameda before the cruise started Mr. Woodward had me lead a crew to clean a space near Radio 1 that I didn't previously know existed. It had a lot of antenna wires leading into it but the room was empty.

No one knows who these guys are and they take their equipment with them when they leave. No one is allowed in the space where they are, and few know where it is anyway. They do not live with the rest of the ET's and do not associate with anyone in any of the ET shops, they had a chief who was the only one to talk to anyone and that would be if they needed something like parts, etc. Almost no one in OE Division knew who these guys were except Mr. Woodward. As far as I know they did not hang around the shops or with anyone, no friends. Maybe, like their specialized equipment, they brought their friends with them. To be clear there are CT'O' types for Operators and CT'R' types for equipment repair, ET's. My understanding is that CTO's are generally language experts.

Later in life I knew a CT that could speak absolutely flawless Korean. On the phone he could not be detected even by the most discriminating native Korean speaker, could speak like a cab driver, an ROK Army Major or a college professor. He was a big guy from Texas. I had friends in the Korean community that were thoroughly amazed at his ability, nice show but I knew what he was in real life.

On Yankee Station Again

VF-154 Black Knights F4J moving on the CAT, VA-155 Silver Foxes A4 next in line

A4 Skyhawk leaves the forward port CAT

A7 Corsair II and RA5 Vigilante on the waist CAT's

The Lone Ranger

Before the cruise started the new Captain brought a full-size white plastic horse onboard and a complete Lone Ranger outfit, guns and all. The *Ranger* always played the William Tell Overture over the loudspeakers when we were pulling away from a supply ship or tanker, or when the occasion was right. But now we had a white horse, saddle, Lone Ranger and all. I heard the 'duty' of dressing up and sitting on the horse at the appropriate times was the purview of the PAO, Public Affairs Officer, the most junior officer. Later I heard there was actually an enlisted man who took over the duty. It was impressive and got a lot of attention. Good times.

Ranger departing Pearl Harbor
Can you spot the Lone Ranger?

Every ship had something, one of our destroyers had the 'Roadrunner' painted on the bridge and when they passed by sounded their horn, toot, toot.

The Lone Ranger seem to be photo shy, there are not many photos of him.

Combat operations started right after we arrived on station in early December. That is what we were there for and we got right to it, sitting around in the computer room waiting for something to malfunction. Well maybe there was more to do.

Food

During the three years I was in *Ranger*, 67-70, the *Ranger* won the 'Best Large Mess Afloat' award every year. The food was great and people often ask about it and I just say "imagine your favorite restaurant", now eat there every day, four times a day and nowhere else, of course, with someone else selecting the menu items of the day. Now you know. I really loved the bread that was made in *Ranger* when we were out at sea. *Ranger* also had a donut machine.

Once when *Ranger* had some DOD visitors I was assigned to escort one of them around anywhere he wanted to go. When it was time for dinner he said he wanted to eat with the men and wait in line too. Maybe he used to be in the army...so we were waiting in line when some of the guys behind us were wondering what was on the menu. One of them went forward to see and returned with the news that it was "Steak and Lobster again!" The DOD visitor didn't know what to think and asked me about it, I remember saying something like 'often enough maybe'. I quickly pointed out that we had 'Chicken Fried Steak' more often.

Overall there was a great effort by the galley crew to make things as pleasant as possible. For a time Wednesday evening was Italian Night. The guys that wiped the tables and kept things clean wore red plaid aprons that matched special tablecloths for the occasion, the menu was Italian and very good as I recall. One of my favorites. I think you could still get 'Chicken Fried Steak', maybe with a little Marinara sauce, on Italian Night in case you skipped it the night before.

A few weeks before we made our annual port call to Hong Kong in early 1970 a few of us were having dinner and commenting on the food. DS2 Ron Hammers said the one thing he missed was the third shaker on the table, he said growing up they always had a shaker of garlic salt as well as salt and pepper, his French heritage. We suggested that he put a note to that effect in the 'suggestion box' which he did. We all laughed but, amazingly, when we pulled out of Hong Kong there were three shakers on every table, one was garlic salt! Maybe I remember this because who ever heard of success at the suggestion box.

It is that kind of care that gets you the 'Best Large Mess Afloat' award three years running.

Holy Helo and the Donut Machine

On Sundays Father Quinn, *Ranger*'s Catholic Chaplin, would fly in one of our helicopters to the smaller ships in the taskforce. Destroyers and other smaller ships did not have Chaplains of their own. My understanding is the services were sparsely attended in the smaller ships. I was told only about 15% of personnel in *Ranger* attended services. Perhaps about the same as the general population, unless you live in Alabama.

During the last homeport visit *Ranger* received and installed a brand-new large capacity donut machine. Every division in the ship had a 'donut card' and someone was responsible for picking up the donuts for that division and carting them to the various offices, etc. Usually the night crew performed that 'chore' and had the first pick of the donuts. It was very popular to say the least. Who doesn't eat donuts?

With that in mind Father Quinn, in order to improve attendance at services, packed the 'Holy Helo', as it came to be known, with boxes maybe crates of donuts. Then Father Quinn flew off to visit all the small ships in the area. I heard he was most welcome and that attendance was, so to speak, heavenly.

It seems, as I recall, that we always had good weather on Sundays, maybe it was the prayers.

Another time when we crossed the International Date Line we had Sunday two days in a row. No excuse to miss services! Many thought Chaplin Ford, the Protestant Chaplin, and Father Quinn lobbied the Captain for that schedule.

At Sea, Replenishment Operations

The Routine of Carrier Resupply Operations in the Tonkin Gulf

Typically *Ranger* was on a schedule that repeated on a four-day rotation for replenishment or resupply operations in the Tonkin Gulf. The flying schedule varied with combat requirements. The ship was on a fairly regular schedule day or night opposite the flight schedule, depending on requirements, we could be alongside a supply ship three days out of four. For example, day one, alongside an oiler taking on 6 million gallons of NSFO (Naval Special Fuel Oil, constancy of tar) from a fleet oiler, the next day taking on bombs and ammunition from an ammunition ship, the third day taking on food from an AK.

USS *Sacramento* AOE-1

One day I happen to be on the bridge when we were taking on food and got a look at the shipping manifest, tons of meat...so many thing I can't remember exactly but one thing stuck out and I do remember it well, thought of it many times, making calculations... six thousand dozen eggs every four days! Think about it, makes sense after a while, 5000 guys, 3 -4 eggs a day just for breakfast, making bread, *Ranger* had the best bread when we were deployed, cakes, donuts, and everything else eggs are used in. If the eggs have bright yellow yokes they are very fresh, if the yokes are dark orange the eggs have been on the supply ship for a while. You learn these things in the navy!

Bringing across 'six packs'...of 500-pound bombs

AOE-1, USS *Sacramento* and AOE-2, USS *Camden* were unique because they could supply fuel, ammunition, and spare parts and were as large as a WWII Battleship and fast enough to keep up with the carrier task groups. They have their own helicopters to deliver some of the freight. Lots of forklifts driving around on the ship.

Line em up, pallets of six each 500-pound bombs waiting to come over
NSFO or JP5 Jet fuel hoses in place

Some supplies come by air, USS *Rupertus* DD-851, Callsign **TEMPEST**, in the background

Handling a six pack of 500 lb. bombs coming over, these guys work hard
...our pilots will make the final delivery

USS *Hollister* DD-788, Callsign **SKIJUMP**, comes alongside for fuel

Refueling one of our escorts USS *Hollister*

Christmas 1968 Online Yankee Station, second Christmas in the combat zone

Second Christmas on Yankee Station, second New Year's celebration in Subic, same show different year. As I recall Christmas time was fairly quiet on the war front, not much going on. Carolina's Rum soaked fruit cakes were a big hit again as every year.

Aircraft Accidents

USS *Forrestal* Legacy

At the time of the fire on the USS *Forrestal* in August 1967 navy aircraft were equipped with ejection seats that can eject the pilot safely from the aircraft when necessary while flying. The problem is the booster rocket under the seat was not strong enough to eject the crewman high enough for the parachute to open if the aircraft was on the ground. Pilots were killed and injured on the Forrestal because they could not get out of their aircraft.

After the Forrestal fire the ejection seats in navy aircraft were updated with a larger rocket boost under the seat and it will get the air crewman high enough for the parachute to safely open even if the aircraft is parked. Don't try this at home.

Launching an F4

The F4J Phantom as normally configured with under wing external fuel tanks, two Sparrow III, and two Sidewinder missiles weighs 52,000 pounds. It was written in chalk on the 'takeoff weight' space near the nose. I walked by them every day going to chow. The F4 is a high-performance fighter plane that is basically two J-79 jet engines wrapped in sheet metal. By today's standards it doesn't fly well at low speeds and glides like a brick if the engines quit. Consequently it requires the extra effort to get in the air. The catapults along with the F4 at full throttle with afterburners is what it takes to get the aircraft to about 160 to 170 knots in the 1/25th of a mile of the catapult length. The 30-knot wind down the flight deck helps but isn't necessary, *Ranger* once launched an F4 while tied to the pier in Sasebo, Japan. I remember at least once while alongside a supply ship taking on provisions we launched an F4. It was quite a show for the ship that was alongside sending provisions over. It surprised me as I sat in the computer room and heard the CAT go off. They just push the CAT a little harder.

VF-21 Freelancers
F4 Phantom on the
CAT ready for
launch

The Switch

I am trying not to tell more than I know here. As I understand it, in the F4J there is a switch that can be set or not set generally by agreement between the pilot and the RIO. If the switch is set, then if one crewman ejects the other will automatically be ejected as well in a carefully timed sequence as to not collide in the air, not at the same instant. If the switch is not set, then each is on his own but I think it still doesn't allow both to go at the same instant.

These incidents occurred over the three deployments I had in *Ranger*, not all in one year. There were other aircraft accidents with other aircraft types that I do not remember as well.

The nervous RIO

F4's fly better in cold weather than in the hot weather off Yankee Station. In cold weather the air is denser. I am guessing the switch was not set when, off Yankee Station, an F4 launched and started to falter, slipping and sliding a little like they sometimes do. The duty of the RIO during the launch is to be ready to get out if things go bad. In this case the RIO must have thought things were going really bad and he blew the canopy and ejected! The pilot recovered the aircraft and came around and landed back on the ship, wind in his face, old school, open-cockpit. The Helo fished the much embarrassed and wet RIO out of the water, he just missed landing back on the ship in his parachute.

F4 bridle failure

When the aircraft is on the Cat for launch it has a bridle, or harness cable, that attaches the aircraft to the 'Shoe' on the catapult. This bridle detaches from the aircraft and is left on the ship as the aircraft launches off at the end of the catapult run. In the case of the F4 there is more rigging but I will not go into that since it has no bearing on the story. These bridle cables are only used for a limited number of launches to insure they will not fail.

When an F4 is on the Cat with everything connected and is ready for launch the catapult Shoe is behind the front landing gear of the aircraft. I think mostly this is true of other aircraft as well.

Apparently the switch was not set again when an unfortunate incident occurred. An F4 was launched and halfway down the 1/25th of a mile catapult run the bridle broke, the shoe accelerated and kicked the front landing gear out from under the aircraft. The aircraft went nose into the flight deck and screamed down the remaining catapult run and off the front of the ship, starboard side, forward, still under full afterburners. The RIO ejected very quickly and was saved but the pilot did not, maybe he was stunned or was having trouble understanding what was happening, hard to say. The plane went off the front of the ship and hit the water, the ship hit the plane and we never recovered the pilot or any part of the plane. It was over so fast. Only the RIO survived floating down in his parachute.

Bad day near Korea

The planes were flying pretty well in the cold weather near Korea, F4's were going straight out without even a little sink off the CAT. Then we launched an F4 and just after it left the CAT it began to lose control and fishtailed some and began to sit on its tail. It was clearly out of control as it started to roll to the left, when it got to 90 degrees the RIO ejected and the aircraft continued to roll when the pilot ejected not quite straight down. From the timing some said they thought the switch was set and the ejection was automatic.

The RIO's parachute opened just in time to hit the water but from what I remember he was, maybe hurt, but OK. We stayed in the area for hours searching and hoping that the pilot might be recovered. After a while it was clear that he was gone and we had to move on.

The pilot's body was recovered nine days later, pulled up in a Japanese fishing net. The pilot was still in his ejection seat but had been decapitated. We sent a recovery party in the helicopter to get him. As I recall one of our Chaplains went on the helicopter.

The A7 accident

For safety reasons only persons that were authorized and trained specifically to be on the flight deck are allowed to be there during flight operations. I was not one of those guys. I did learn some of the rules for being out there though. One rule is not to step on anything but the deck. Keep your feet on the deck!

With that in mind, we were launching a major daylight strike, all the aircraft had been launched and the last to go was an A7 Corsair II that was on the forward port CAT. The bomb arming safety wires had already been removed and the A7 was ready to launch, jet run up, CAT officer signaling. The pilot signaled a no-go. The CAT officer signaled the crew a no-go and the process of getting the A7 shutdown and moved began. The 'Red Shirts,' the bomb guys, got started putting the safety wires back in the bomb fuses on all the bombs on the aircraft. Right side completed; a Red Shirt started to walk around front of the A7 to the port side of the aircraft. The yellow tow bar had already been attached to the front landing gear and was stretched out in front of the A7 waiting for the tug to arrive and move the aircraft.

Meanwhile the A7's engine is still running and the CAT officer is still giving hand signals to the pilot. He finally gives the signal to shut down, the pilot revs the jet and then kills the fuel, standard procedure, just as the Red Shirt walks around the front of the aircraft. It is safe to do this as long as you stay outside of the yellow tow bar, the measured distance, and keep your feet on the deck. Stepping up on the end of the bar puts you in the air intake vortex. I saw the PLATT, shipboard video system that always watches the flight deck, replay several times. The Red Shirt was sucked through the air and directly into the A7 air intake as soon as he stepped on the end of that tow bar.

The engine was already being shut down when this happened so there was nothing to react to. He was unconscious from head trauma, his helmet broke, and he suffered broken arms and collar bone, as I recall. He was taken to sick bay and, upon diagnosis, the Captain immediately ordered the COD transport plane to be configured to carry a stretcher. He was transported as soon as they could to the big Naval Hospital at Da Nang. I heard he passed away a day or two later.

Follow the Leader

When anything out of the ordinary happens in the ship, it gets around through the grapevine, especially in CIC. On this occasion two F4's, I am certain they were *Ranger* F4's, were returning from a mission over Vietnam. They were short of fuel, called 'low fuel state' and requested a straight-in approach due to the fuel state. The shipboard air controller stated that he did not have them on radar. The lead F4 pilot said that his TACAN showed him approaching the ship. The air controller stated he still did not see them on radar. The F4 pilot said he was approaching the ship and would be flying over in seconds. He looked down and realized he was flying over the DLG that was running 'South SAR' many miles from *Ranger*!

'South SAR,' Sea Air Rescue, is a Guided Missile Destroyer that patrols between Yankee Station and the southern part of North Vietnam. It is one of the ships that can intercept North Vietnamese aircraft that may try to strike the carriers operating on Yankee Station and it also coordinates rescue operations for down pilots.

My understanding is that sometimes strike aircraft heading into Vietnam will tune their TACAN air navigation equipment to the South SAR TACAN as a waypoint on the way in and on the way out from a strike. One F4 was following the lead plane and apparently not doing any navigating on his own. The lead plane had the South SAR TACAN tuned in and failed to retune to the *Ranger* TACAN. They were over a point way short of the *Ranger*.

When this error was understood *Ranger* immediately launched the 'Alert 5' tanker and it raced toward the 'low fuel state' F4's as the F4's were on a course toward *Ranger* and conserving fuel.

The tanker plane, an A3 'Whale', had the F4's in sight when their tanks went dry! Four pilots ejected and went into the water. As I recall no one was hurt and the helicopter picked them up but two F4's in the drink. They were probably too busy trying to stretch fuel to recheck the navigation settings. Do your own navigating, I always say! I would love to be 'fly on the wall' during that debrief.

"The Sea stalks the unwary and relentlessly pursues the careless".

The Dog Fight

The computer room is right next to the Combat Information Center and as such you might say is close to the action. One day one of the RD's (radar operators) stuck his head in the computer room door with a 'something is hot' comment. So a couple of us went into CIC and stood in the far corner out of the way by the 'IC3' display console. The IC3, 'Intercept Controller 3', console would only be manned if the entire Chinese air force came down on us, so it was a good place to be out of the way and watch what was going on in CIC and on the display console.

There are a lot of details here to be recalling this many years later but this is close. The *Ranger* and *Enterprise* were operating together in the Tonkin Gulf and conducting strikes into Vietnam. Both carriers had two each 'BAR-CAP' F4's (Combat Air Patrol) in the air to protect the ships, so that is four F4's in the air.

Radar, probably from our E-2 Hawkeye, showed some 'bandits', North Vietnamese MiGs heading toward Yankee Station and avoiding the DLG at South SAR for what might be a clear shot at the carriers. Rest assured there is no such thing. We were watching all on the display console. I do not remember exactly but I think it was six MiGs, a big strike, generated lots of attention in CIC. Seems we never see that many MiGs in one place. The four BAR-CAP's were vectored to intercept but were ordered to hold short and wait for the launch of the Alert-5 F4's from each ship. This would also include the tankers because fuel is an important issue when starting into a dogfight.

The *Ranger* Alert-15 F4's were ordered launched. Now we have 8-10 F4's milling about smartly waiting to go in after the MiGs. At this point some of the MiGs turned and ran but one or two continued the run in. Before any of the F4's engaged, the remaining MiGs raced in and let lose all their missiles then ran for home.

Two of the *Enterprise* F4's were hit and went down, four pilots in the water! They were all OK, as I recall.

When an F4 goes to combat speed and drops the wing tanks (clean wings) it has about 16 minutes flying time. I was shocked at how short that would be in combat until I found out that is about 10 minutes longer than the MiG has!

Another 'fly on the wall' opportunity missed to hear the 'after action' report on that incident.

EC-121 Incident, North Korea Again

It is "déjà vu" all over again this year. It was the *Pueblo* Incident last year and now the North Koreans are at it again.

On 15 April 1969, the North Koreans shot down an unarmed radar surveillance plane, an EC-121. That is a four engine 'Super-Connie" with a radar dome on top. Again we redeployed to the Sea of Japan area from Yankee Station.

I could see what was coming and talked to some of the CIC guys who relayed my suggestion to the CIC Commander. I recommended that before we went to EMCON-A and went radio silent that we get the operating information for the Korea area. CIC was a very busy place. I was interested in the radio frequency for NTDS Link-11, probably the last thing on anyone's mind. That way we could see what was going on up there while in transit and in radio silence. In some ways it seems incredible that a DS2 in maintenance would be the one to suggest this. You had to be there, all the officers and operators in CIC were extremely busy on so many things. I know from the year before they would have waited too long to think of this. I got an 'atta boy'.

Tuned up the SRC-16 on the correct frequency before EMCON-A was set. Even for receive only the SRC-16 takes 125 Watts of forward power to initially tune the antenna multi-couplers in the final stage of phasing and loading into the changing conditions on the antenna. Part of being able to stay hidden and still see the tactical situation in the Korea area as we approached depended on setting up the SRC-16 on the correct frequency beforehand for the Link-11 data link and getting the DLRP, data link reference point, for the area. The two pieces of information that mattered.

When EMCON-A was set the radiomen were putting all their transmitters in standby, standard procedure. I had to keep them away from the SCR-16, if they put that in standby mode it would disable the receivers. Link-11 was put in 'receive only' in CIC.

On the way to Korea we were able to monitor the tactical situation both in the Tonkin Gulf and the Korea area and still be in radio silence.

The USS *Enterprise*

When *Ranger* arrived in the Korea operating area Lt. Woodward called me into the EMO office and told me the NTDS Link-11 in the USS *Enterprise* was down. Yes, the *Ranger* and the *Enterprise* again this year. None of the four channels were working. The Admiral was riding the *Enterprise* and was upset because the data link was down, they were blind. Lt. Woodward told me to go to supply and take what I thought I might need and fly over to the *Enterprise* and 'fix it'.

I went to supply, knew exactly what I wanted, filled a sea bag with everything but the kitchen sink. Took the Helo over to the *Enterprise* with all my parts, in all the excitement I forgot my extra clothes and my camera. Good thing I took my brain.

When I got there it was easy to see the problem. The guys working on the SRC-16 were in way over their heads and knew it. I asked if there was anyone actually trained on the SCR-16, they said there was but the chief had put them on other duties as part of a cross training program. The SRC-16 has four transmitters and receivers referred to as 'channels'. In about two hours I had two channels up but the Link-11 was still not up because the SSQ-29 data terminal was also down, I wasn't expecting that.

I went up to the computer room where the SSQ-29 was and found the problem quickly and the *Enterprise* was on the air.

The *Enterprise* was a 'mess'. They had a chief who believed in cross training everyone but didn't understand at all about the new digital electronics, to him a transmitter was a transmitter. I was in their EMO office writing my maintenance report when that chief came in with a basket of tubes. They were from the AN/SPN-10 analog computer for the automatic landing system. He said the technicians claimed they were bad and he tested them on a tube tester and they were all good! I thought 'you total idiot'! I told their EMO that no one in their right mind would pull all the tubes out of that system and mix them up. They were all from analog op-amps that were very sensitive and now the entire system would require a great deal of maintenance to get it working again.

Big disaster, very poor leadership from the EMO and all the electronics officers down to the chief they apparently could not control. To allow a chief to reassign carefully trained technicians that could have solved the problem and send for a technician from another ship while the Admiral waits is a real leadership problem in my book.

I went back to the *Ranger* the same day. Since I was in high school and read about the USS *Enterprise* it was my dream to serve in it someday, now I did not even want to sleep one night in the "Big E". My dream did come true though, I did serve in the USS *Enterprise*. Careful what you wish for, right!

DLG at GQ

One night during the EC-121 incident someone came into the computer room and said things were getting hot in CIC. So of course, we slipped over to CIC and stood quietly in the corner near the IC3 console which was rarely manned. It was nighttime and apparently one of our helicopters had spotted some debris in the water and was in the area searching for more, as the story goes. In any event there was a Russian freighter, as we could deduce at the time, that was actually firing on the US Navy helicopter. I do not know the names of any of these ships.

The admiral was in his underwear on the other side of CIC talking on the 'red phone', the encrypted radio communication with a Guided Missile Destroyer (DLG) in the area. We could hear the captain of the DLG on the speaker, he was stating that the DLG was at GQ, battle stations, and was at flank speed approaching the area and within sight of the Russian ship. He also stated that the "Cease and Desist" order to stop firing had been sent several times in the clear and via semaphore, light flashing, but Russians were ignoring it.

We were also watching the IC3 NTDS console at the time and saw the ships in question displayed and could see the DLG had weapons systems locked on the Russians. The Admiral asked the DLG Captain if he had 'guns' locked on, meaning the 5-inch main gun. That was affirmative and the Admiral said send the semaphore signal one more time and if no answer then fire one round across the bow of the Russian to get their attention.

Just then the Russians quit and turned off course and retired from the area. Guess they didn't like a DLG charging in at full speed flashing "Cease Fire or be Fired Upon".

Russian Overflight

Some stories are a little technical to relate, this may be one of them but here it goes. Off Korea, when the initial stress of the EC-121 incident was calming down the Russians decided to try their hand at overflying *Ranger*. In other words send a long-range reconnaissance bomber to fly over *Ranger*. They like to see if they can do it, a big game of brinksmanship. This is something they would never play at in the intensive combat zone off Vietnam. The Sea of Japan area is very close to Russia.

Jim Hill PH2

Tag, you're it, *Ranger* F4 escorting a Russian Bear bomber - long range reconnaissance plane

We have two long range radars in *Ranger*, the SPS-30 which can spot a high flying aircraft out to maybe 500 miles but paints a faint video on the scope and the SPS-37 which is a low frequency radar that can see a couple hundred miles out and paints a great 'big banana' video on the scope, a great favorite of the radar operators. There is also the SPN-6 radar, shorter range, and can see sea skimming targets out 50 plus miles. All of these Radars are watched all the time…in theory.

A Russian Badger long range bomber approaches hundreds of miles away, he is operating his radar, looking for us, presumably, and he is 'radiating' all his electronics. Electronic

Countermeasures sees his radar before he sees us and even before he comes on our radar. The fact that he is approaching directly on our bearing merits excitement in CIC. Soon enough he is on the SPS-30 Radar and then the SPS-37 Radar. At this point the normal CIC SOP, Standard Operating Procedure, for operators goes out the window, porthole if you can find one. As all the radar operators' switch to the SPS-37 for a good look at the approaching Russian. Due to the type of signals radiating from the Russian plane ECM has it ID'd as a 'Badger'. He was flying at 20,000 feet. 'Piece of cake'.

Two F4's were dispatched to fly out and get on his wings and get him turned around before he can get within 50 miles of *Ranger*. This is SOP. The two F4's get out there and take some nice photos...at 20,000 feet and the Russian turns around. They didn't notice the other Badger that was flying directly under the first Badger only this one was skimming the ocean all the way in 'on the deck' with no electronic emissions. Radar didn't see him because the SPS-37 was painting the 'big banana' on the high flyer and masking the low flier! Everyone was tracking the departing Badger. The SPN-6 would have picked up the low flier...had anyone been looking at it! The second Badger was spotted by the bridge lookout as it flew toward and directly over *Ranger*. What an embarrassing day! 'Atta boy' for the bridge lookout.

"The Sea stalks the unwary and relentlessly pursues the careless".

Man Overboard, Sadly, Accidents Happen

With around 5000 men, more ammunition than a fleet ammo ship, and more fuel than a fleet oiler, care is the word. I am sure this took place off the coast of Korea and I believe it may have been February 1969 during the EC-121 incident.

It was nighttime and *Ranger* was taking on ammunition, mainly 500LB bombs. When we take on bombs, 500LB bombs in this case, they arrive on steel pallets of six each. The bombs are separated from the pallets and taken below to the magazines. The steel pallets are then sometimes banded together in stacks and passed back to the ammo ship. Sort of recycling. Sometimes they are just discarded over the side into the ocean. In this case, there may be several reasons why, cold weather, darkness, extended time alongside the ammo ship, hard to know, but apparently it was decided to toss them overboard.

Everyone was dressed in heavy coats, cold weather gear and gloves. As the steel pallets stacked up a forklift drove them to the other side of the hangar bay where the port side aircraft elevator was lowered to the hangar deck level. Two seamen were assigned to push the stacks of pallets into the ocean. All was going as usual when, as they pushed one stack of steel pallets over the edge of the aircraft elevator one of the seaman got his glove caught on the stack as it went over and he was dragged off the aircraft elevator and into the ocean. The light pinned to his coat was on, some said, but he quickly disappeared and was not recovered. Every effort was made to find him. *Ranger* was moving slowly, around 10 to

11 knots during the Unrep process. He was not on the surface.

In the cold waters off Korea in February if you fall into the water and you are well dressed you have 5 minutes until you are unconscious and maybe 10 minutes until you are dead.

Think tank and NTDS Link-11

Think tank and NTDS Link-11 unencrypted, early 1969

Apparently around spring of 1969, time approximate as much as I remember, the navy had a suspicion that the tactical information being sent over Link-11 was being read by the enemy. This is one story about how they proved it. It involved the USS *Ranger* and that included me, the small cog spinning in a very big wheel. Among other things I was in charge of maintenance of the NTDS Link-11 data communications system.

Link-11

Let me begin with a description of Link-11, a bit technical but will help to understand what happened and what a seemingly impossible task it should be for anyone to read the data.

Link-11 was a digital data communications system that linked computers on NTDS, Naval Tactical Data System equipped ships and aircraft such as the E-2 Hawkeye ATDS, Airborne Tactical Data System, the P-3 Orion and the MTDS, Marine Tactical Data System ashore. Sort of like the internet only over radio. Operationally in the Gulf of Tonkin in Vietnam we used it ship to ship and ship to air with the E-2 Hawkeye, and MTDS. We did not normally 'talk' to the P-3's or have any ASW, Anti-Submarine Warfare contacts displayed on NTDS consoles. The Pueblo incident is the only time I know of where we displayed the ASW contacts but there could have been others. Submarine locations, any submarine locations are considered highly classified.

Various data was transmitted on Link-11 including radar tracking information, fire control status, weapon commitment to which targets just to give you an idea. It was all 'tactical' information and presumably most useful if you could get it in real time. In a way who cares what you were looking at yesterday, of course there is always the study of after battle progress, so all information new or old is important.

Technically, binary data from the NTDS computers in 24-bit words was sent to the AN/SSQ-29 data terminal equipment (modem). The SSQ-29 employs a modulation technique called Collins Kineplex which uses 16 tones starting with 605Hz and 15 incrementally higher tones in the audio band of 300Hz to 3 kHz. The tone package of 16 tones is broadcast in frames of 13.3ms where each tone, except 605Hz, is phase shifted from the previous frame in increments determined by the two bits of data encoded into each tone. The 605Hz tone was constant so the entire tone package could be phase shift corrected for Doppler shift that would occur, for example, as a high-speed aircraft is either flying toward or away from the communicating stations. As can be seen 15 tones is 30 bits of data, the other six bits are the Hamming codes inserted by the SSQ-29 so that any data received with a bit in error could be corrected. The entire package is then sent out on HF radio in Double Sideband Suppressed Carrier (DSB) mode. There is more but this is enough to get an idea how hard it would be to decode this as it goes high speed from station to station much like the internet.

The Potter Tape Drive, my SSQ-29 in the background   Logic drawer 3 on my AN/SSQ-29
                                                          Data Terminal equipment

The computer also fed information to Link-14, a secure teletype link with non-NTDS ships so they can see what is happening and plot the tactical situation on their 'grease pencil' CIC plot boards.

Even if you had the raw data it would be necessary to know what it means, how it is organized, who is tracking what, etc. Without knowing the computer end of the data it would be nearly impossible to figure it out, one would think. Anyway, wouldn't you need an AN/USQ-20 computer?

Think Tank, 'The Briefing'

Sometime in early 1969 the USS *Ranger* was operating on Yankee Station in the Tonkin Gulf when we received some visitors. I was included into a very small group that was briefed by them regarding an upcoming mission and the reasons for it. I was told it would involve data communications which is why I was included. In the briefing we were told that the entire documentation for the AN/SSQ-29 Data Terminal, classified confidential, and Link-11 was compromised by a NATO officer from the Italian Navy. When I heard that I remember thinking 'Good Luck' because the Collins Kineplex system with its mechanical filters would be so hard to duplicate, personally I did not think at that time that anyone could do it. We were also told that a magnetic tape containing the classified computer information with everything you need to know was stolen from a civilian contractor out of the trunk of his car at a seedy motel near Mare Island. Real spook stuff, seedy as it gets. I found it hard to believe that all this was connected. Probably there was more and we didn't need to know it.

I will try to get this right as I can remember 50 years later. The USS *Ranger* was operating on Yankee Station in sight of the usual "Chinese Junks", fishing boats that often tried to get in our way as we started to launch aircraft. The destroyers kept them at bay but Electronic Counter Measures and our own 'spooks' had the 'Junks' transmitting messages every time we launched aircraft. So we know we were watched and every move reported.

The Operation

The operation went something like this. One of the programmers from the 'think tank' installed a 'patch' into our bank of NTDS computers to allow a selected track to be falsely moved in whatever direction we chose and the false track information would only be sent on Link-11 and not anywhere else including Link-14.

Jim Hill PH2

VAW-115 Liberty Bells, E-2 Hawkeye, the Airborne Radar ATDS Link

With an E-2 Hawkeye already in the air and operational we launched five F4J Phantoms in full sight of the 'junks'; the Phantoms went to altitude, presumably so they could be seen on enemy radar, and we tracked them correctly on NTDS. At a point where the E-2 could see there were no 'junks' or any enemy ability to visually see what is happening at low altitude, one of the F4J's dropped to the deck way below anyone's radar and proceeded away from the area on a clear path where no one could see him on the sea or on radar except the E-2, of course, and they were not sending track info on that F4. The actual track for that F4 was not broadcast on Link-11, instead his broadcast track was shown on Link-11 only, to be penetrating Chinese airspace over Hainan Island at treetop level.

F-4J moving up to Launch, 'Junk' in background...watching and reporting

Through the E-2 over NTDS we all had a ringside seat as the Chinese Air Force scrambled to intercept the false track. They took the bait. Damned exciting stuff. I had not believed the Chinese could do it, but I did then.

When the *Ranger* returned to NAS Alameda at the start of summer 1969 I was sent immediately to Crypto school and new equipment called the KG-22 was installed in *Ranger*. When we went back to the Tonkin Gulf in November 1969 every NTDS ship we operated with had encrypted Link-11. I was the 'Honor Man' in my crypto school class. I was really paying attention to the 'spook' stuff now.

The flight of the Intruders

Zero – Zero Visibility

This is one of those interesting incidents that happens onboard ship. Not anything to do with me. The A6 Intruder is a great aircraft, the A6 can get off the flight deck with a bomb load greater than a WWII B-17. I always thought it resembled a bumblebee.

I am not sure when this happen, I think it was Cruise 8 or 9, and I am not sure where, Tonkin Gulf or Sea of Japan. It may have been during the EC-121 incident, Cruise 8 off Korea, 1969.

In OE Division as electronic technicians and computer technicians 12 on 12 off was the usual workday but with nowhere else to go we worked longer; few persons slept more than six hours in 24. If something critical broke we didn't sleep, the price you pay for having a relaxed schedule like 12 on 12 off. I worked inside the ship below decks and might normally never see outside but I made it a point to go through the hangar deck to the mess decks for chow each day. This gave me a chance to see outside through the deck edge elevator doors and to pass close to the aircraft. I like airplanes. The weather in the Tonkin Gulf was almost always perfect, hot and humid, but nice. In any event in *Ranger* with our great weather group if we didn't like the weather we would just move. In the Sea of Japan and the Yellow Sea off Korea things were different especially in February, any February.

It was a quiet late night with no flight operations when someone came into the computer room and said we were going to trap aboard two A6 Intruders in zero zero visibility using the SPN-10 automatic landing system in Mode 1A. I couldn't imagine where they were coming from because *Ranger* was not flying any other aircraft. In any event I headed up to "Vultures Row" to see this in person. The flight deck is the 04 level, "Vultures Row" is on the island structure about level 07 this is the only place where any crewmember can go to observe flight operations. Normally no one is allowed on the flight deck during flight operations except the flight deck crew. When I got to "Vultures Row" I noticed that it was the darkest night I could remember and the fog, which was very unusual to see at all, was so thick I could not see the port side of the flight deck much less the bow or stern. The red lights were on, even with that I could hardly see the flight deck directly below me.

Two Ranger Intruders, VA-165 Boomers

It was unusually quiet outside as the ship turned into the wind and picked up 30 knots of wind down the flight deck. I could have watched this in CAATC the Carrier Air Traffic Control Center at the SPN-10 console but wanted to see it for real. I could hear the first A6 approaching but could not see a thing, heard him hit the flight deck and grab the wire and the whine of the wire pulling out...then I saw only the nose of the A6 come out of the fog and stop, amazing. The second one came in right after, same show, could only see the nose sticking out of the fog when it stopped. I was thinking this was really crazy. This is why we are the best; no one would dare to land an airplane anywhere at night in this visibility.

Intruder Down in North Vietnam

Another more interesting and exciting incident happen, I am fairly sure during Cruise 8 (68-69), is about another A6. One of our A6 Intruders was hit over North Vietnam and the two pilots managed to bail out. When anyone ejects from an aircraft an emergency radio beacon is transmitted on 243MHz. The alarms started to go off in CIC, I am guessing around 9PM. Before 10PM the Captain came on the 1MC, the ship wide announcing system, and informed the crew the A6 was down. This was rare, usually there is no announcement about these things to the entire crew. He said that he was patching in the conversation with the down pilots so everyone could hear, really not normally done! The down pilots were talking from a walkie-talkie relayed through our E-2 Hawkeye deployed high above somewhere between the action and *Ranger*. The Hawkeye sees all.

One pilot was saying one of them had an injured leg from the bailout and they were hiding in some brush. They said the NVA were looking for them and mentioned they could smell the cooking at the campfires. Just like in the movies the enemy was going through the brush with bayonets stabbing the bushes. They said they would stop talking and wait for 2300Hrs.

At 2200Hrs, the usual time for Taps, the Chaplin and prayers, the Chaplain came on the 1MC and everyone said a prayer that night, probably even the 85% of the crew that never went to services, me included. The 85% number decreases the closer you get to 'fox holes', we were pretty far away from that, but the pilots flew into Harm's Way every day.

We knew their exact location. As the saying goes "meanwhile back at the ranch", the ship became super busy loading bombs and missiles on aircraft readying for massive coordinated strikes on everything in the area. Coordinating with the "Jolly Green" force that would fly in and rescue the pilots. The E-2 was watching everything, CIC was busy as first the tankers launched, then the strike aircraft followed by the fighters. All to arrive on target at the same time. Every target around these guys on the way in and on the way out was about to light up. There was activity in the crew's mess as well, the senior cook, a CS-1 that had been in *Ranger* since it was commissioned was baking a massive cake. Party planning was in full swing.

Vultures Row view of a visiting Jolly Green, rarely did we see one this far out at sea

At 2300Hrs. the conversation started again, few were sleeping, and was on the 1MC again for a few minutes, as I remember, and then the 1MC was switched off as the details were worked out with the pilots.

All went well for everyone concerned except the NVA. The "Jolly Green" carrying the pilots arrived back on *Ranger* in the early morning, as I recall there was daylight. The pilots were taken to the hangar deck where the party was about to start with the cutting of the massive cake. One of the pilots had an injured leg but insisted on going to the party before reporting to sick bay, Carrier Pilots, got to love em'.

I vaguely recall not getting a piece of that cake, there were a couple thousand guys on the hangar deck, I called it a day and went back to the computer room.

Yet another Think Tank and the F4J Phantom II

Sometime in early 1969 I was selected to participate in another troubleshooting group to work with another Think Tank group. The new task was a problem with the ACLS, Automatic Carrier Landing System, bringing the F4J Phantom onboard with Mode 1-A recoveries. See Supervising the SPN-10 Group for more information on the ACLS system. The problem seemed to be only with the F4J and not with the A6's or A7's which also had the system. I thought I was included because I was the senior guy on the Link-4A shipboard digital data link to the F4J, but instead I was sent to the F4J group and some aviation guys were sent to the shipboard system. It turns out the civilians thought all us experts would point to each other instead of solving the problem. So the ace troubleshooters were on the job.

The problem was that when the F4J was in the approach pattern about 15 seconds or so out, just before the pilot would take over from the autopilot at 10 seconds to touchdown, ½ mile from the ship, the aircraft sometimes made a dangerous dip almost hitting the water in a few cases. Makes the pilots very nervous!

I was told there was no stupid question and so I learned a lot about the Phantom. Of course, I saw the data link radio and the autopilot including the switch group that enables it. Interesting stuff. Learned about all the backup systems like the two backup hydraulic systems. It takes 20 minutes to change out a J-79 jet engine. With the aircraft tied down if you remove any skin plates the aircraft cannot be moved or the skin plates may not go back on. One neat piece of information was that the F4 has only one battery...it lights the 'EJECT' light in front of the pilot and RIO when all the backup systems have failed. Time to get out, the F4 has the gliding angle of a brick when the engines quit.

The problem turned out to be an instruction in the NTDS computer program, the 30 bit data word sent to the flap controls via Link-4A on the F4J had some 'most significant bits' OR'd instead of AND'ed with a constant which could abruptly set a more significant bit in the flap control. I knew it was software all along, right!

Tape Recordings and More

Almost everyone bought a lot of stereo equipment in the Philippines and Japan. We had it stored everywhere in the various compartments and behind equipment. Some was set up in the various shops and the computer room. Boyd bought a Sony tape recorder you can see it in the background of the photo "Me and Harry Mckee" on page 54. The Sony had an 'auto-reverse' feature and played that same tape continuously. Three years later on a quiet in-port day when everything was shut down we noticed that it didn't sound so good, we couldn't tell with all the noise out at sea. Upon a thorough check of the electronics, we can do that, it was discovered the tape was worn out and so was the recording head, big grove worn right into the head. Couldn't fix that.

In ET Shop 2 they had a turntable setup with a couple tape decks hooked up at any given time. In those days records were popular and pre-recorded tapes nearly nonexistent and expensive. So we recorded records onto tape, everybody did it. They had a nice turntable but we only recorded when we were not flying, the continuous thump of the catapults and vibration of the arresting gear when a plane was trapped (landed) would cause the needle to skip. Even in smooth sailing the tone arm was set much heavier than you would at home. Where is my penny? I recorded many records there on my super nice Teac 4010 Tape Deck. High quality gear.

When I got home, I set up all my nice new gear in the living room of our nice quiet apartment. I would play my tapes and when I closed my eyes to enjoy the music I felt like I was back in the ship! At first I thought it was the music I knew so well. When I played records I didn't get that feeling. It took a while to figure it out but what happen is the movement and vibrations of the ship, that we all ignored daily, was picked up by the needle on the phonograph and recorded on our very high-quality tape decks. With nice big speakers with plenty of bass, I can still listen to those tapes and be back in the ship. It is nothing you can hear, it is the 'feel' of the ship that you recognize.

After the first cruise I had a nice Sansui receiver and Teac 4010 tape deck at home and Carolina would record hours of KIOI, FM 101 in San Francisco and send the tapes to me. They were very popular, commercials and all. I still have some of them and they do not have the ship 'feel' even though we listened to them many times in the ship.

The Great Water Caper

Almost all of *Rangers* major electronics equipment was water cooled. Inside each radar, computer, major radio transmitters, digital display consoles, etc. were water cooled heat exchangers. Each piece of equipment has a small water-cooled heat exchanger and fans. This allows the equipment to be sealed to outside issues like smoke and fire and remain operating. The DS's were in charge of the high purity closed loop water system since it was mostly our gear that used it. The main reservoir and the main sea water fed heat exchanger that kept the water cold, was in a room of its own. The system was 'closed loop' in that the high purity water was in a closed system and was never allowed to escape. When it did need water we had to carry five-gallon bottles of triple distilled medical grade water from the engine room to the 03 level, about eight stories, give or take!

The water level of the reserve tank and purity were on the preventative maintenance schedule to be checked every week as I recall. We didn't look at it every day and suddenly one day we got a low water alarm! What! We had to carry about 25 gallons to bring it back to proper levels. We looked and looked for any leaks and couldn't find any and the level was staying put.

The next morning we checked again and it was down about a gallon or so but all at once. Carried more water just in case, kept looking for a leak. Next morning, bang, down again. The investigation went on, we started to suspect someone was using the water each morning. We placed people all around in passageways and near equipment to try to find out what was happening.

Svenson discovered there were plier marks on the maintenance tap for the one NTDS Display console on the bridge. Kept watch and found a signalman on the bridge using it to fill a coffee pot every morning. Mystery solved, we informed him in no uncertain terms 'this water is off limits'. It turns out there is no water on the bridge and the Signalman had to go down at least 4 levels to get some, oh well. He commented it made great coffee!

Sabotage!

Suddenly the SPS-37 radar shut itself down with an 'over temp' alarm. The thing is this happen just when a Russian Bear long range bomber was approaching at long range. Coincidence? We did not think so and started an immediate investigation. This could be serious, if it was one of us and was coordinated...maybe by radio! I was close enough to the investigation to know that everyone in OE Division was cleared. That means, if not a coincidence, someone knows more than they should about our systems and we don't know who they are.

During our investigation I was informed that a sailor on another carrier was caught operating a clandestine radio on the fantail of the ship. We knew enough about our systems to know the loss of one radar was not going to blind us but maybe someone else did not know that. Someone had turned the cooling water off to the SPS-37, one of *Rangers* most powerful radars and the one that can see around the earth curvature to some extent, which means detecting sea skimming targets at range.

That valve was located in the passageway on the 03 level just outside the SPS-37 radar equipment room. The valve did not have a handle, someone brought their own! We never did find the responsible party but kept a sharp eye out and questioned anyone loitering around any of our spaces. It could have been just a case of someone turning a knob they should not have. The sticking point is that whoever did it brought their own knob!

Hong Kong 1969

When we visited Hong Kong in 1968 a bunch of us went shopping. I bought a lot of stuff including the top of the line Singer sewing machine for Carolina which I actually used on the ship to sew on patches for some of the guys. Three of us walked into a small Hi-Fi store and the owner was very friendly. He invited us all into the back room for tea, it was a really nice time, very relaxing to be treated in such a way. We must have stayed for hours; we did purchase some things. I think I bought my Garrard turntable there. I have to admit that we were very suspicious at first but quickly realized he was just a nice proprietor.

I never visited a bar in Hong Kong, no shore patrol for me, I cashed in my IOU's for all the shore patrol I did in Subic.

I walked into an ivory shop one day and saw lots of things carved out of ivory. I saw a very large dragon carved out of a single elephant tusk and mounted on a wooden base. It was impressive with a ball carved in the mouth of the dragon, not removable. All one piece. The closer I looked at the checkered skin of the dragon I saw that under the skin inside the dragon was an entire war scene, knights, castles, horses, soldiers the entire length of the dragon from behind the head to the tail. Unbelievable artwork. I asked the price and the guy told me $6,000HK which was $1,000US. I didn't have that much money and couldn't, more probably wouldn't borrow it. I figured at that price it would still be there the next year, lots of things in the store looked like they had been there a long time.

I set aside, little by little, the thousand dollars and when we visited Hong Kong in 1969 I went immediately to that shop. The dragon was gone! I inquired and was told it sold to a Honolulu businessman only two weeks before! Oh well.

In those days it was still legal to import ivory, it never occurred to me where it came from, the problems of killing elephants was not in the headlines until many years later.

Seth, ET-3... Cruise 8 and 9

Seth was a nice enough guy, an average technician, but could not seem to set priorities. In those days I never heard of attention deficit disorder, ADHD, and probably not many had. Seth would be diagnosed as one today for sure. He was an electronics technician and didn't work for me of course but was a fixture in the ET Shops 1 and 2. ET Shop 2 was close to the computer room and the DS's often hung out there with the ET's.

One day we got a call on the intercom in the computer room asking if we saw Seth. Almost 100% of the time enlisted men called each other by their last names, but Seth was Seth. I answered that we had not seen him in the computer room at all that day. What is the problem? An hour ago Seth was sent from ET Shop 1 to ET Shop 2 to pick up a part and bring it back and had not been seen since. The trip should have taken 5 minutes maximum each way.

We started a search of the passageways between the shops, the computer room was between the shops but nearer to ET Shop 2, all on the 03 level. I started from the computer room heading forward in the starboard 03 passageway searching and I came across a guy with a clipboard and some tools and dirty clothes like he had been working on something, seemed to me that he didn't belong. We always interrogate persons that don't belong since we had one incidence of suspected sabotage. I asked him what he was doing and he replied that he was opening and inspecting some of the large ventilator shafts. He admitted he was from down below, engine rooms, and didn't know his way around, was just trying to identify and inspect the shafts. He told me that someone had come along and he asked that person for help. The said person not only helped ID the correct shaft but was in the shaft actually performing the inspection for him. I called into the shaft "Seth". It was him.

Seth was with us for Cruise 8 and 9 and then his enlistment was up. He wanted to re-enlist but Lt Cmdr. (LCDR) Woodward blocked him. Mr. Woodward told me later that after Seth got out of the navy he went home to Portland where he tried to re-enlist but Mr. Woodward had blocked him permanently.

The Atomic Toilet

The 'Head', navy for restroom, showers, sinks, toilets, etc., for the sleeping compartment for OE Division, ET's and DS's, was about frame 231 near the aft end of the ship on the port side. It had easy access from the outside catwalk just below the flight deck. It was the responsibility of OE Division to maintain this Head even though many crewmen from the flight deck also used it.

The toilets were flushed from the high-pressure fire main with a pressure reducer, of course, to reduce the pressure to a reasonable level. There came a day when the pressure reducer failed on one toilet. This causes the water to literally hit the celling when flushed! That toilet was taped off with masking tape so no one would use it. We did have panels between toilets but no doors. Stall doors would not be good on a combat ship.

As fate would have it, Seth was sent back to begin the process of preparing the Head for painting. He started chipping paint and sanding and finally came to the toilet stalls. He removed the tape and started cleaning and sanding. Then it was time for chow or some other distraction so he left and an unknowing person from the flight deck came down to sit, had his book with him. One of our guys came in and at first wondered if that toilet had been repaired and then just as he was about to say something the guy reaches back and 'courtesy flush' for the last time! The water blew right through his legs on its way to the celling pushed him off the toilet and sent the book flying! No good deed goes unpunished!

The Big Sleeping Contest

I guess it was just one of those days when the ET's tired of playing cards, smoking and drinking soft drinks when someone had the bright idea of holding a sleeping contest. In 'OE' Division we had DS's like myself that maintained all the electronics gear and computers associated with the NTDS computer system. Then we had electronics technicians and they came in two general varieties, communications equipment maintenance from ET Shop1 and radar and associated equipment's from ET Shop2. It was the ET's in Shop 2 that thought up this idea. The DS's frequented Shop 2, probably because it was closer to the computer room.

So, as I heard, the contest rules were that a participant had to stay in bed, only getting up to go to the rest room, period. No getting dressed and going down to chow. Just stay in bed and sleep. I do not recall how many participants there were, maybe five or six at first. Any more than that may have been missed for duty. I know some of the guys were taking food to the 'sleepers'. Hard to remember but the 'sleepers' became fewer and fewer until the last guy lasted a week I believe.

As I recall no DS's were involved in this and no animals including ET's were hurt!

Back to the War

Finally after more 'line periods' on Yankee Station it was time to go home. As I recall we left Subic for a swing past Yokosuka Japan to meet the relieving carrier. Probably more motorcycles with the same proviso that if we were to be recalled into combat the motorcycles go over the side along with anything else that gets in the way like Hi-Fi equipment. We weren't worried about that; our stuff was crammed into classified equipment spaces.

VF-21 Freelancers, armed with two Sparrow III and two Sidewinder air to air missiles

The typhoons between Hawaii and Japan seem only to exist in November when we are headed over, smooth sailing back to San Francisco Bay in June.

Return Home to NAS Alameda

Another great homecoming. Carolina met me on the pier with a couple thousand other wives and sweethearts, just like in the movies. Wonderful times to be had by one and all.

Red Right Returning

When a ship is returning to port the rule is 'Red Right Returning' which simply means keep the red buoy to your right to stay in the shipping lane. It was common practice on *Ranger* to use the 5-inch gun director radars at low power on the port and starboard side of the ship to track the 'Green' and the 'Red' buoys respectively as an aid to maintaining position in the shipping lane. *Ranger* had a very tall mast and it was important to enter the San Francisco bay at just the right point and maintain position. The top of the *Ranger's* mast is 173 feet from the waterline which can vary depending on loading of the ship. This is the height of the TACAN Dome, the topmost antenna. A few times we waited out at sea for the right tide as well before entering SF Bay. A move not popular with the crew, of course.

The gun director radars, normally used to direct fire of the 5-inch guns on *Ranger*, could be powerful but were used in a low power mode when navigating the SF Bay.

Many times when entering SF Bay birds are resting on the buoys but this time a bird was destroyed in what I heard was an obvious case of high-power radiation. It was like the bird was shoved into a microwave oven and exploded! Needless to say the investigation looked first at the gun directors. Before long they got wind that a couple guys were bragging they had locked the SPS-30 radar on the buoy and cranked up the power. The SPS-30 radar was, at the time, the most powerful shipboard radar in the navy at 6 million watts and the operating frequency would have been correct for a microwave oven. It was originally designed as the tracking radar for the TALOS missile but was also a great high-power long-range air search radar. It has a tracking ability, if it is purposely 'locked on' to a target, like the buoy, at that short of range anything on the buoy would be in a high-power microwave oven.

As I remember a couple of guys did get into trouble for that. The navy frowns on that type of behavior, bad PR. I do not think they were ET's or maintenance personnel; I seem to remember they were a couple of RD's, radar operators.

Long cruise, ready to go home...by the way, get a haircut!

CHAPTER 11

Summer of 69

RAV at Hunters Point:

This homecoming was looking good, the ship would be serviced for the next three months at Hunters Point Naval Shipyard across the bay from Alameda. So I could be home most every night. How nice! This was a great summer, finally, to be home with Carolina! The best summer since 67. I took the launch, shuttle boat, from Alameda to Hunters Point every morning and returned every evening that I didn't have duty, four section duty, stay on the ship 1 day out of 4. I also attended two schools at Mare Island during the summer and was home every night.

Ranger in Drydock at Hunters Point, CA

They had to put *Ranger* in drydock and pull off one screw which also means one of the rudders had to come off too. The screws, four of them, are 35 feet across and weigh 13 tons each. Last year after the RAV when we were leaving the Puget Sound we hit a floating log and it went through the screws hitting one of them causing a very minor dent.

Unfortunately this 'dent' caused *Ranger* to have a slight acoustic noise that could identify the ship to enemy submarines. We had to go on Cruise 8 with it that way, no choice. Now it needed to be fixed.

The hinge pin for each rudder is 36 inches in diameter, a 36-inch hole had to be cut in every deck starting at the flight deck all the way down to the rudder drive motors so a crane could 'pull the hinge pin'. In the photo notice the guys on the scaffolding going into the side of the rudder to disconnect the pin. After the screw was replaced and hinge pin re-inserted, the holes had to be re-welded. To re-weld the hole in the flight deck, ceiling of the hangar deck and hangar deck, all three special armored steel, copper bars were welded on first and power hooked up to heat the area to something like 300 degrees before it could be welded. I was told that only about 100 guys in the US could weld that grade steel. In any event it was so hot they had to wear special suits and be relieved often. I was watching them when I had a chance and asked questions. Talk about an electric bill!

Crypto School

Off to Mare Island. Graduated 9 July 1969 from the TSEC/KG-22 school, was 'Honor Man' in the class. Certificates for both, nothing else to say.

AN/USQ-36 School

Back to Mare Island August 1969 to attended school on the AN/USQ-36 which was a newer version of the AN/SSQ-29 which we had on the ship. A new USQ-36 was installed in *Ranger* for a second data link, Link-21, for the IOIC group. I would also be in charge of maintenance for that system too, just the data communication part.

While I was attending the USQ-36 School, my brother, Jerry, was in town on his way to Vietnam as a helicopter pilot. He had a few days to visit before flying out of Travis AFB. One day we planned to go somewhere right after class so Jerry sat in the back of the classroom. The instructor OK'd it, Jerry was in uniform. Some wondered what an Army WO was doing in class for the day.

CHAPTER 12

The Third Deployment Starts

Third Deployment, Cruise 9, 1969-1970, 14 October 1969
Captain J.P. Moorer

Mid October 1969, off again. This would be my last deployment in *Ranger*, although I did not know it. Carolina's sister, Rose, came from the Philippines to stay with us. It was great and now someone would be with Carolina while I was away. Rose would attend her senior year at Alameda High School. It was a really great summer together.

Hated to be away from Carolina again. Life was great but in some respects I was somewhat anxious to just get going…almost as if leaving sooner would get us back sooner.

Problems with the Primary
High Frequency Antenna

Departed 14 October, on the trip from Alameda, CA to Hawaii for the Operational Readiness Inspection. In route we encountered a problem with our primary HF 2-6MHz antenna. This was a serious issue. It would require a lot of work in the shipyard to repair it and probably delay our deployment by at least a few days. Anything that affects the schedule of a major ship like USS *Ranger* demands a very high priority for repair.

This may be a bit technical again but let me explain. *Ranger* had many radio communications receivers, mostly in 'Radio 1' and twelve HF (High Frequency 2-30MHz) radio transmitters in 'Radio II', eight AN/WRT-2 SSB transmitters and four that were part of the SRC-16. There were also a few AN/WRT-2 transmitters in 'Radio III' but they were not a problem because each was on a separate 22-foot whip antenna.

A radio transmitter is not much good if it is not hooked to an antenna. The SRC-16, my gear, had a very sophisticated system of antenna 'multi-couplers', it could connect any of twelve HF transmitters to any of three main antennas, 2-6MHz, 6-15MHz, and 15-30MHz. The 2-6MHz broadband antenna was the main antenna in use because that frequency band had the greatest ability to transmit long distances and the SRC-16 could put eight transmitters on it at the same time. It was an 'End Fed Inverted V' long wire antenna that went from the top of the island to the top of the mast and back down. As you can imagine, with airplanes you cannot string a long wire antenna just anywhere like you can on some ships.

A couple days out of Alameda the 2-6 Broadband antenna developed an electrical short in the transmission line to the antenna. Since all the transmitters in Radio II were connected to the SRC-16 I was in the spotlight. I employed a number of troubleshooting practices including disconnecting the antenna base feed box and the SRC-16 end of the cable. I determined there was an electrical short in the main cable leading to the antenna. Because of the seriousness, this was confirmed by a number of people looking over my shoulder including two ET chiefs. When an ET chief confirms that you have a short in your Heliax, you have a short in your Heliax.

After confirming I had an electrical short I used a TDR (Time Domain Reflectometer) to find out how far the short was from either end. I found it was 40 feet from the SRC-16. That placed it partway up the Mast alley inside the mast with many other cables. A close inspection of the cable showed no signs of damage. A TDR sends an electrical pulse down the cable and measures the time it takes for the pulse to be reflected back from the short thus giving the distance to the short. Pretty sophisticated piece of test gear, the only time in 50 years of experience I ever used one, but we had one in *Ranger*, got to love that.

The real problem is this is not just any old cable but 2" diameter sealed Heliax, with equipment to keep it nitrogen pressurized. Heliax is just like a pipe with the center conductor suspended by a spiral nylon spacer. The theory is some piece of metal could have been in there from installation and gradually worked its way to a position where it shorted the inner conductor to the outer conductor.

Due to the length of Heliax and the immense difficulty in replacing it this was a serious matter. The short was checked and rechecked and reconfirmed by senior technicians other than myself.

An emergency order was sent to Pearl Harbor regarding the problem and they should be ready to replace the Heliax immediately on *Rangers* arrival. LCDR Woodward (now Lt. Cmdr.) arranged for me to fly in ahead of the ship to Pearl Harbor to work with the shipyard and have everything ready when the ship docked. As soon as *Ranger* got close enough to launch the helicopter, I was on my way to Pearl.

When I arrived at the shipyard planners' office at Pearl Harbor I learned that the only roll of that special Heliax was in Florida and was at that moment being loaded onto a 'C-141 Star Lifter' for a direct flight to Hickam Airforce Base, next to Pearl Harbor. Just the thought of the expense of that made me nervous. The shipyard was arranging for a tall crane to be in place to hold the roll of Heliax so it could be pulled down from above. Crazy! I always referred to it as "two man" Heliax" because it would take two men with a pipe bender to put even a small bend in it. This was going to be a herculean effort to thread this down through the mast alley and compartments to say nothing of removing the existing Heliax.

The USS *Arizona* from the helicopter on the way to Pearl Harbor ahead of *Ranger's* arrival

Photo of the USS *Arizona* I took when flying into Pearl Harbor ahead of *Ranger*
'Battleship Row', November 1969

I was waiting with a couple shipyard engineers when *Ranger* docked. We boarded right away; this was priority one. We started by confirming the problem but now could not find any short! The shipyard engineers were upset and accused me and others of not checking this out thoroughly. Two officers and two chiefs said they rechecked it themselves just before the ship arrived and the short was still there! Saved my butt on that one. Everyone was doubting themselves and going over their processes.

Now what to do, replace it or take a chance that it was just something that has been in there for two plus years and just now showed up and then because of the ship's movement relocated out of the way. The decision was made to go ahead with the ORI and reevaluate in three days after the ORI. Meanwhile remain prepared to replace the Heliax if the problem showed up again during the ORI. After the ORI the problem still had not reappeared and the decision was made not to replace it and go to war as is. The problem never reappeared but I was always watching for it. Technically something rattling around in the Heliax could temporarily reappear and fault out some transmitters and then disappear, but I never saw even that happen.

Tug pushing *Ranger* away from the pier at Pearl Harbor, November 1969

USS *Ranger* CVA-61 departing Pearl Harbor, Hawaii, November 1969
Lone Ranger on deck, the two smokestacks of the Waipahu sugar mill in the background

On to Yokosuka, Japan and the War, *Ranger* gets in gear, wide turn out of Pearl harbor

Blah, Blah, Blah, Blaaaaah, that is the sound the NTDS Link-11 transmission makes if you listen to it on a radio receiver. One day I had business in Radio 1 and I heard that sound on every receiver in the room, the RM chief was complaining about it. I told him I knew what it was, it was my data link. He wanted to know why it was on every frequency after about two weeks at sea. I knew. It is not something the normal radio guys see. I explained the Link-11 transmission is a phase shifted 16 tone multiplex package that is transmitted in 'double sideband, suppressed carrier' mode and the salt crystals that form on the antenna insulators after about two weeks at sea make nice non-linear diodes. The rectification and 'mixing' across this non-linear circuit at these power levels is causing all the 'splatter', as it is called in radio jargon.

After that I noticed the radiomen cleaning antenna insulators in all kinds of weather every week or so. I didn't see him much but that chief always had a smile for me. With RM chiefs that's a win.

A quick stop in Yokosuka Japan to take on 'special weapons' from the relieving carrier and then off to the war.

An Officer and a Gentleman

Sometime during the second West Pac Deployment, 68-69, I met a seaman sweeping the passageway outside the computer room. He asked if 'we had computers in there' and I said we did, why? He explained he was a high school math teacher and computer programmer. I wish I could remember his name and his photo did not make it into the cruise book, good friend though. To make a long story short he was assigned to OI Division, radar operators, awaiting an appointment to Officer Candidate School (OCS). As a seaman with no prospects of being there very long you sweep the passageways and any other odd job. Super good guy, Mr. Woodward agreed to have him transferred to OE Division and he became one of us the rest of the cruise.

Of course, the guys took him to Olongapo when we docked in Subic to hit the bars. I shook my head. When he came back once he related that he met this very well-educated Filipina girl that had a degree in chemical engineering, his degree was in mathematics. He said he didn't believe her and spent the next couple hours interrogating her to see if she was for real. He said she was. Most of the guys weren't interested in talking or, for that matter, in chemical engineers. I guess they did enough talking out at sea.

Apparently, she was much more of a business person and not really spending time in bars and it was a chance meeting. In any event he arranged to see her anytime we were in Subic, much as I heard. At the end of the cruise back in Alameda he was off to OCS.

Fast forward to the 69-70 West Pac Deployment, *Ranger* was in Subic, we were sitting in ET Shop 2 during the day and suddenly we hear "Attention on Deck", said by the first person to see an officer enter the room. As we all stand up at attention and turn it is our brand-new Ensign newly assigned to the Naval Station Subic Bay and his very beautiful Filipina chemical engineer wife. It was really great to see him and everyone swarmed around him even though he was an officer now. Fairytales do come true! Life is great.

CHAPTER 13

The Odyssey

Orders to the 117AHC, Long Binh, RVN
Adventures "In Country"

On June 26, 1969 my brother Jerry, 2 years and nine months younger than me, graduated from the US Army helicopter flight school, received his wings, warrant officer W-1 appointment, orders to Vietnam, and turned 19 years old all on the same day.

Jerry was assigned to the 117th Assault Helicopter Company at Long Binh, RVN to report there in September via Travis Air Force Base. I would be leaving in October for my third deployment. That left some overlapping time and we had a week together in Alameda before he had to report to Travis AFB for transit to Vietnam.

I was finishing the USQ-36 transition course at Mare Island and *Ranger* was at Alameda. Jerry and I had a good time together before he had to leave. We wanted to stay closer in touch, by November we would both be in the combat zone at the same time but, of course, in very much different roles.

In early December I talked with LCDR Woodward and, on a lark, broached the subject of visiting my brother as the Christmas season was just around the corner. Amazingly he said he would look into it. He got back to me quickly and said he could arrange TAD orders to Jerry's unit; you have seven days! Wow! Careful what you wish for.

Had to get my shot card up to date for the trip so I went down to medical where my good friend and favorite corpsman, Tom Clemans HM2, was in charge of shots. He told me I needed this really bad shot in the butt that would protect against Hepatitis. I told him I didn't have enough time to recover from that, I'd still be hurting when I got back. I talked him into marking it on my shot record without the shot but he said if I got sick I should tell them I didn't have it. He also mentioned if you get captured "you will be up shit creek without a paddle". I made a note, don't get captured. Things were looking up.

With my 'side arms authorized' orders to the 117th AHC, I left the ship headed for Da Nang on the COD, the C-1 aircraft *Ranger* used for general transportation. I had only a general idea of how I might navigate my way from there to Long Binh in the middle of the war. I was dressed in a Marine fatigue uniform with shoes, not boots, and a USS *Ranger* ball cap with the PO2 insignia on it, looks like an eagle to army people. I was more in costume than a recognizable uniform which probably helped because once I left Da Nang no one knew quite what I was. I know some only saw "RANGER" on my cap and some only saw an "Eagle". I stayed the night in the transit barracks at Da Nang, very exciting. I wondered if it was an omen.

In a ship you learn to move immediately when certain things happen like simply sudden silence, sudden silence is always a bad thing in a ship. "Fire, Fire, Fire", or "General Quarters, all hands man your Battle Stations" over the 1MC, often follows. A sudden silence may precede a fire alarm for that area because the power was shut off before the fire alarm was announced. That few seconds could mean survival in some cases. Remember *"the sea...relentlessly pursues the careless"*.

So there I was just settling into a bunk in the transit barracks a little past 10PM, the lights were out, when the "RED ALERT" siren went off, I jumped up into my clothes, just like GQ on the ship, and when I hit the door I fully expected to be the last one out but to my amazement everyone, to the man, had not moved. Then I heard a voice from the darkness "Where are you going?" I said it was a Red Alert, the voice came back "That is for the other side of the base, this is the Navy Side". I didn't want to appear ignorant so I said I would go sit on top of the shelter bunker and watch.

The guy was sort of right there was an attack some distance away and it seemed pretty heavy but what do I know. Then the one and only rocket, someone said it was a rocket, managed to whistle in and hit the unoccupied barracks two buildings over from ours. The guys came running out of the transit barracks like crazy and I had my revenge, I said "not to worry, the rocket hit two barracks over". Big commotion but no one was hurt.

Bien Hoa Airbase

The next day I left early and managed to get connecting flights all the way to Bien Hoa Airbase next to Long Binh. It was not easy because clerks kept saying it would take a week but I bluffed my way at least once just because they didn't know what my uniform was. Within hours I made it to Bien Hoa on a C-130. I was in the air terminal and asked someone where the 'Head' (rest room) was and he pointed to a door, I went through the door and was outside...there was a row of 'port-a-potties'. A real classy place.

I was instructed to walk to the main gate, not far, and have the sentry flag a jeep for a ride to Long Binh. I did and he did and during the ride to Long Binh I thought to myself "I sure am glad it is not my job to shoot people because I see many guys standing around in black pajamas and funny hats, holding AK-47's" looking like bad guys to me. It turns out they are simply local constabulary. If I had been assigned, instead of being a visitor, 'in country' Vietnam I would have had an official indoctrination and would know these things.

The 117th AHC

The guys in the jeep drove me right up to the headquarters for the 117th AHC and for the first time I had a stroke of apprehension. What if they say "what the hell are you doing here", after all this was not coordinated at all. I was not expected, I took a deep breath and marched in. A sergeant was at the first desk, I said I needed to report in and, without asking a question, he directed me right away to the major in the next room. I reported smartly at attention to the major and presented my orders. To my amazement he was quite happy about it, said it was great, "welcome aboard". He said Jerry was out on a tough mission at the moment and that he had been flying tough missions for a several weeks in support of three battalions of Cambodian mercenaries around Bu Dop, near the Cambodian border, and that I should just take it easy and walk around and wait. The major also said he would assign Jerry to some 'milk runs' for the next five days and I could fly with him! How good is that!

Waiting for Jerry to return I walked around the flight line and saw a couple guys working on something so, of course, I went over...they were disassembling a rocket warhead that had not functioned properly and there were thousands of 'flechette' darts pouring out, they looked like nails with fins instead of a head. The guy asked me if I wanted some, 'take a handful', so I did. I gave them away to people for years, there is only one left on my shelf now.

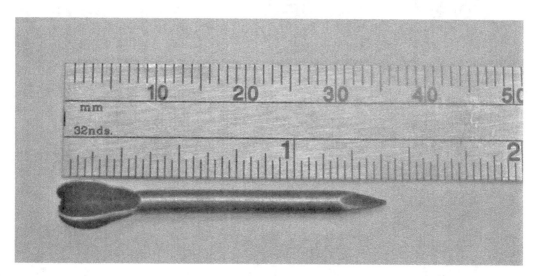

My last Flechette from Long Binh

Probably standing around when someone is taking a warhead apart was not a good idea, my first indication was they were away from any buildings or aircraft. You think of these things later but I was getting smarter.

These rockets are fired from a helicopter gunship and are referred to as 'Nails'. They have 10,000 steel flechettes in the warhead along with high explosives and a radar proximity fuse that sets them off 30 feet from the ground when fired. It is said that if people are closely packed into a football field size area and a gunship puts a pair of 'Nails' into the target everyone gets hurt. The 'Heavy Hogs', Cobra Gunships, routinely go out armed with 19 pairs of these rockets.

Jerry arrived that evening and I got billeted in the 'Officers' Country' with Jerry. We went to the officers' club and had a couple beers. The next day we went flying on the "Milk Runs", right, very exciting. A family war, just Sergeant Smith's kids at it again. I just turned 22, Jerry was 19.

'Officers Country' at Long Binh, not exactly shipboard accommodations

All of our missions were flown out of the Navy PBR (Patrol Boat, River) base at Nha Be. We would fly from Long Binh to Nha Be in the morning and fly assigned missions out of there.

Day One

We ran a couple missions out of Nha Be, nothing special as I recall. Just like a taxi service. Spent a lot of time looking at the Vietnam countryside, nice and green. As we flew along I noticed the banks of some of the rivers were denuded back from the water a couple hundred yards on both sides with Agent Orange to prevent ambushes on the river. After they sprayed that stuff there was only mud. Couldn't help wondering what something that powerful was doing to the water, just a thought at the time.

Jerry loading up for the day's mission, ready to preflight the aircraft

Anybody call for a Taxi? A remote base we flew into

US Navy Hovercraft at Nha Be

Jerry and I getting ready to go on a mission, in my Marine uniform with '38' in shoulder holster
The white T-Shirt has to go, too good of an aiming point I guess

Day Two

Jerry asked me if I would like to fly the Huey, of course! Both of us used to fly, dad had a private pilot's license and we flew many times growing up. Jerry got his private pilot's license at 16 years old, we used to fly when I was on leave. Of course, I had many hours flying uncle Franks J-3 Cub before joining the navy but I never went for the license.

At the officer's club I noticed that Jerry's hand shook a little, like a nervous twitch, when he picked up his drink. I mentioned it and thought to myself it must be rough duty for Jerry to be nervous. He commented that it was nothing.

I climbed into the right-hand seat; Jerry got in the back. The other pilot took off and when we were airborne and flying straight and level at altitude, he told me to take over using just the stick and pedals, he would handle the cyclic.

I held the stick tight and it didn't move but the helicopter was all over the sky. It turns out it was not a nervous twitch but the required 'feel' for the controls of a Huey! Guess you need flight school for that one. I did fly a combat helicopter in the war, well for ten minutes anyway. That was all they could take.

We got to a 'free fire' zone and I shot the 'Ma Duce', M-2 50 Cal Machine Gun and the M-60 machine gun. We were flying the only Huey in the unit that had a '50' mounted on it. Normally they have an M-60 machine gun on each side. We tried our hand at throwing some smoke grenades, which was harder than it looks in the movies. I got close to the target; timing is everything. Lots of fun, especially firing the '50'.

Jerry and I on the ground at Nha Be, me in WO flight suit now keeping the '38' in my pocket

Day Three

"Bad Moon Rising"- Creedence Clearwater Revival.

The door gunner had some business to take care of so instead of replacing him it was decided that I would be the door gunner for the day. After all the first two days were so uneventful, what could possibly go wrong, 'milk runs', right!

I didn't expect to actually have to shoot at anyone but I was definitely prepared to do just that without hesitation as the situation may arise. It was on my mind and I recall having no problem with it. I knew if that became the case someone would probably be shooting back and that didn't bother me either. Sort of the psychology of the time. To be clear, not a hero, just no fear as such.

Again we had the Huey with the '50' on one side, the crew chief had that and I was on the M-60. We headed for Nha Be, unbelievably cool! When we got there a mission was already planned. We took on a USMC Major and a Vietnamese marine with at least three radios on his back and handsets hanging down over his shoulders, a regular walking 'Comm' center. We were headed out to scout a certain area in the Delta.

When we got to the area the major said on the intercom there was a boat (sampan) that was in the wrong place and we needed to turn them around. We flew over them and the major used a megaphone to yell at them in Vietnamese but they didn't even look up, we tried again, no response.

Then the major said have your gunner put a few rounds in front of the boat! I could see there was at least five people in the boat including maybe three children. If he said they are bad guys, hose them down, that would be easy from a gunner prospective, just follow the tracers. Of course, he would not say that in this case because it was obvious they were a family. The point is I didn't have enough experience to miss. I am a good shot but I only fired an M-60 once in my life and that was the day before and it is difficult from a moving helicopter.

Anyway I led the boat some ridiculous amount and the M-60 fired one round and jammed. I cleared the round and I heard Jerry tell the major that the gun was giving us trouble and the crew chief should fire instead but the major said no, give it one more try. I did and it jammed again. This time the crew chief fired the '50' and the bullets hit right in front of the boat so close the water splashed on the first person. That got their attention. They turned around. That was too close. So much for the 'milk runs'.

By the time that 'Bad Moon' was rising Jerry and I were back in the officers' club having a beer, maybe still the beginning of a charmed life, too early to say.

After the first day I always wore the WO Flight suit because it made it easier to eat with Jerry in the officers' club at Nha Be. Carrying a sidearm into the enlisted chow hall at Nha Be was a hassle, so eat at the officers' club I always say.

Day four

We had the gunner with us again and I rode in the back, out of the way, as usual. I was dressed in a Warrant Officer Flight suit, no one asks questions or tries to give you orders. We headed for Nha Be. Shortly after we landed a couple of navy seals, very young and innocent looking with neatly pressed uniforms, came out and said the pilots were needed in the briefing room. I waited with the gunner and crew chief as usual.

Hovercraft from Nha Be headed out across the Song Nah Be River in the Mekong Delta 12-69

In about 30 minutes Jerry and the other pilots returned, two helicopters, always two. Jerry said maybe I should stay here for this one. I really didn't want that...to be stuck on a navy base dressed in an army WO uniform, what if he didn't come back! A lot of explaining to do. I said I didn't care what it was I wanted to go. I think Jerry glanced over at the other pilot and got a nod and I was OK'd for the flight. Get in the back!

We got in and started engines and then it became obvious why he wanted to leave me there. We took on two Huey loads of navy seals and Vietnamese marines really loaded for bear, guns, ammo, mortar, grenade launchers, camouflage, face paint and all you can imagine, very serious guys. I remember having my camera but didn't take a photo, didn't know if they would consider it bad luck and wasn't about to ask like some tourist. Many military guys are superstitious. These guys were going to kill people today, I didn't want to interfere. The mission was to insert the team into an unsecure LZ in daylight. Word was they would stay out all night to ambush the bad guys.

As we got close the gunner told me to get on the M-60 and he grabbed a CAR-15, carbine version of the M-16, from the back. I told him I was a good shot with a rifle and not as good on the M-60, as demonstrated the day before, but he said it would work fine and if I heard shooting I should immediately press the trigger and look for a target in that order.

We only got close to the ground and these guys were out of the Huey and into the jungle in a flash. No shooting, we got out of there in a hurry so as not to give them away.

The M60 probably would have worked fine there. My main problem the day before was the speed of the helicopter was whipping the ammo belt in the wind and the ammo would not feed properly into the gun, thank God. There was a K-ration soup can clipped on the side of the M-60 to help it feed ammo but it didn't help me. Of course the real gunner knew how to handle it.

Hovercraft at Nha Be, really liked the mini-gun with spade grips

Day five

Was fairly uneventful, mostly taking passengers from here to there. No more seal teams or marines. The most interesting was when we took an army major to a remote village that looked just like the camp in the movie 'Green Beret'. We landed close to the camp and shut down; the major was there for a meeting. While we were waiting an army sniper approached and said he wanted a ride to another location, no problem. We didn't actually talk to him, he did all the talking, said he was out in the jungle alone for three weeks. Said he got a 'niner', we fished-in and asked what is a 'niner' and he told us he shot nine bad guys in a row coming across a dike without anyone knowing they were being shot at. Shot from back to front, an accepted practice since Sgt. York in WWI. Never shot from inside 300 yards, lived in a tree at all times and changed trees every day. A bizarre character, had sort of a gleam in his eye, seemed to me to be enjoying his work a little too much. We also took on an Australian army medic who was taking care of the people in the local villages, the only non-asian guy around. Finally, the major came out and we continued on the rounds.

Waiting in line for takeoff, mission out of Nha Be, that's Jerry

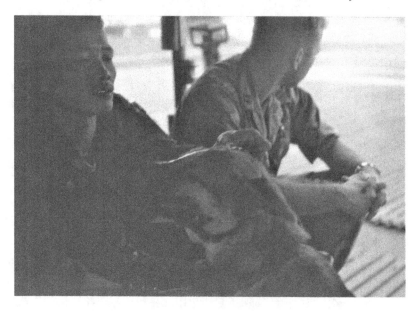

Another passenger, Marine Captain and his faithful dog and handler, tough guy
talking about the dog of course. Recognized me right away as a dog person
smart dog, the muzzle stayed on

The real 'Door Gunner', notice the soup can clipped on the side of the M-60, helps prevent jams
It didn't help me much, when it comes to M-60 machine guns – Smith you are just a klutz
'Stick with what you know'

Flying in support of an operation

Going back

After five exciting days of flying Hueys it was time to return to *Ranger* and get my sanity back. Amazingly, right out of the blue, the major said, "If the navy can send a man in here then I should be able to send a man out to the ship" and he cut orders for Jerry. I didn't know what to think, wondered what the *Ranger's* Captain was going to think. I am sure the major considered it R&R, Rest and Relaxation, I think Jerry got five days maybe more.

We caught a C-130 from Bien Hoa to the US Navy base at Cam Ranh Bay and I spent the night in the transit barracks. Jerry had to bunk at the BOQ. The navy was also a stickler about letting me into the officer's club with Jerry, they didn't appreciate my costume, so we went to the enlisted club and they almost didn't let Jerry in there because he was an officer but finally relented. We had a beer. The navy is very formal about these things, the army was OK with it. The next day we got a hop straight into Da Nang.

Getting to the *Ranger*

The Naval Air terminal at Da Nang was very crowded with guys trying to get everywhere and trying to get to *Ranger*. Getting back to *Ranger* was doubly compounded by the fact that the Bob Hope Show just wrapped up on *Ranger* again this year. I didn't get to see this one. The jam up at Da Nang with the Bob Hope Show was that during the show period, for days, the personnel and mail destined for *Ranger* was stacking up. I inquired at the desk about getting to *Ranger*, they said "days"! The planes were outfitted for mail and only one passenger per plane, "Take a Number". Jerry and I had two- or three-digit numbers in line.

On *Ranger* most of the CIC officers among others were also pilots. To maintain their flight pay and hours they would fly the 'COD', *Rangers* C-1 transport plane, on occasion into Da Nang. Incredibly, I spotted CMDR Uelman, *Ranger's* CIC Commander, I went up to him, he was very surprised to see me and said "Smith, what are you doing here"? I introduced Jerry and related a short version of the story and said Jerry was sent to visit the ship but we are in a long line and running out of time.

CMDR Uelman immediately arranged for Jerry and I to have the seats on the next two flights leaving very soon...he was flying the first one. I put Jerry on the first flight with instructions on how to get to the EMO Office when he got to the ship. I didn't want to chance things going wrong if I left him behind. He left with CMDR Uelman.

The COD's normally have several seats in them but in this case they were outfitted for carrying mail with a net that cordoned off all but a small path from the entrance in the rear of the plane to the cockpit. *Ranger* only has one COD but with so much mail backed up they were shuttling extras. In this configuration two pilots facing forward and behind them a partial separating wall and two seats facing rearward. One seat for the enlisted air crewman and one seat for a passenger. Hence only one seat per plane for passengers when configured for carrying cargo or mail.

Jerry left for the ship first and when he got there flight operations were underway and they had to circle until it was clear to 'trap' aboard. After he was aboard someone took Jerry to Vultures Row to watch me come in, during the wait a plane, maybe a 'cold cat', went in the water, pilots punched out, parachutes, and helicopter rescue, plenty of action. Jerry always said he was a little nervous after that, wasn't sure the carrier was that safe a place to be after all. He also knew he would have to take off again in a couple days! "How's the water"?

Then it was my turn, one of the other CIC officers was flying the C-1 'Triple Nuts' as we called it, I went on that. I was seated behind the pilot but facing aft and on the left side looking down the small corridor to the entrance at the back of the plane. The air crewman was seated facing aft but he can see only mail, there is an opening between so we can see the pilots and see out the cockpit front window if we turn backwards. OK, so we are flying merrily along toward *Ranger* on Yankee Station and I am numb with boredom basically looking down at my feet and sometimes out the window at the sea.

Jim Hill PH2

The *Ranger* COD, 'Triple Nuts' December 1969

After quite a while I noticed a small fire extinguisher, the type carried on aircraft, laying loose by the back door. I thought "that should be secured" and then thought what is going to happen to it when we hook the wire and suddenly stop? I tried to get out of my stupor, it wasn't easy sitting facing backwards wondering what happens when we suddenly stop, will my glasses fly off? All this time I was thinking I should just get up and secure the damn thing, but I didn't. Finally I realized that it was going to come at me at about 60 or more miles per hour, I immediately turned to look out the front to see if we are getting close to *Ranger*. Thinking I would run back and secure it. Looking out the window of an aircraft a ship on the ocean never looks bigger than a dime...maybe a nickel. I turned and looked out the front and saw the mast then the flight deck up close! No time! I turned back quickly and put my feet up, thinking if I am lucky it will stay on the deck and pass under. We caught the wire, that fire extinguisher launched right off the deck, flew the length of the plane and hit me flat on the bottom of both feet right where my knees would have been. The air crewman saw it and went white, it was his responsibility to secure it. I signaled that I would not say anything. I could still feel the sting 20 minutes later. Remember *"The sea...relentlessly pursues the careless"*.

Jerry and I on Vultures Row back on *Ranger* and back in my real uniform 12/69

By the time I landed and got to the EMO office Jerry was being escorted around and having a good time. There was no trouble, it turns out the captain's son was also an army helicopter pilot. Had a good time, uneventful good days, then Jerry launched on the COD and went back to the helicopter war.

Between returning from *Ranger* to his unit and September 1970, during that first tour, Jerry was shot down four times and got his first 'Bronze Star' along with many 'Air Medals'. He turned 20 on June 26, 1970. Jerry would do one more tour in 1971, receive a 'Silver Star', another 'Bronze Star', two 'DFC's', and the rest of 48 'Air Medals', and get shot down five more times in six months but flying OH-6 'Loach' Gunships this time.

We didn't mention to mom and dad that we were both flying in the same helicopter in combat until Jerry and I were both safely back home. Dad was not surprised.

19-year-old helicopter pilots were not that unusual at the time. The army started with the best and the brightest and sorted out those with the 'knack' then put them through the world's toughest helicopter flight school and right into combat. Fly where "Angel's fear to tread" and be great at it! Dangerous work, not for the meek. More than half the pilots of Jerry's flight school class were killed that first year in Vietnam, 69-70.

Oddly enough it takes 12 months from enlistment to graduation to train a helicopter pilot, some helicopter types take longer, and about the same time to train an Electronics Technician, add ten months more for a Data Systems Technician, very different skill sets, of course. All of these programs have very high standards for acceptance. It takes more than desire to get in and more to get through it. It starts when you are six years old, Jerry always wanted to fly and I always wanted to work with electronics. We were not 'wishing and hoping', we were both doing it from a young age. We both had the 'knack'.

Life at the 117AHC...from a Navy Prospective

Just some of the things you notice when you are accustomed to living in a ship and then suddenly you are in the army!

The 117th AHC (Assault Helicopter Company) was just one of many units contained in the giant US Army base at Long Binh, Republic of Vietnam. The base was reportedly surrounded by 19 rows of fencing with mines, claymore mines, machinegun guard towers, dogs and seismic detectors sensitive enough to detect someone digging with a spoon and, of course, lights. Still the enemy occasionally gave it a try and I understand sometimes succeeded!

One night there was a 'Red Alert' and Jerry and I went out to the shelter to watch. There was a cobra gunship working out on the fence line quite a distance away from us. It was interesting to watch the cobra firing its mini-gun. Firing 'five ball one tracer' ammunition at 2000 rounds a minute it looked like a solid line at night. I would see the line appear and then sometime later hear the brrrrr from the gun. Count the seconds seeing the line of bullets to hearing the sound to know how far away the gunship was. At 1130 feet per second, it was pretty far from us. No rockets this time.

More 'Officers Country' at the 117th AHC

I ate in the 'Mess Hall', army for galley, and the food was good, they served a great breakfast. It was like trying a new restaurant in the neighborhood but *Ranger* food was better. One thing struck me; the army had great milk. In *Ranger* unless we were near the Continental US we had reconstituted milk, powdered milk prepared as required, I could not think of a good reason to bother with it, much less pour it on a perfectly good bowl of cereal. Word was the army had a large dairy plant to make the milk. All I can say is they had good milk…couldn't tell it from the real thing.

I got to stay with Jerry in 'Officers Country' where the Officers were billeted. I normally would have to stay in the enlisted barracks. At least the officers had hot water, I understood the enlisted barracks did not. This was definitely not shipboard accommodations 'Officers Country' was constructed of rag-tag wooden boards and half tent like rooms, more or less. A lot like camping out with some extras. They were referred to as 'Hooches'. In the daytime when we were out flying young women know as 'Hooch Maids' came in to clean up, wash clothes, shine boots, etc. The hooch maids were constantly supervised and all had background checks by the Military Police, etc. to be qualified to work there inside the base and in the officer's billets. The officers considered the hooch maids untouchable, completely off-limits and made sure they were treated well and paid well.

One more difference, in the navy I did not have a submachine gun or a '38' revolver hanging in my locker and we shined our own shoes.

Hey, I don't have one of these in my locker   One of the 'Hooch Maids'

CHAPTER 14

Back Online

Christmas 1969 Online Yankee Station, third Christmas in a row in the combat zone

We had the little tree again in the computer room, still didn't take a photo of it. Carolina's fruit cakes, dripping with Rum were still very popular, naturally I saved some of them for myself.

New Year's celebration in Subic again for the third year in a row. Did some more shore patrol duty. When out with buddies and had some fun too. 1970 was shaping up to be a very busy year from here on out. Little did I know.

Carolina's Mom and two youngest sisters, Chit and Kathy, came to Olongapo from Cavite near Manila to visit with me. Tom Clemans and I went to the house where they were staying in town to see them. We had a very nice time.

Lynn and Chit, Dec. 69

Carolina's Mom with Chit and Kathy, Tom Clemans and I

Super Bee Reconnaissance Drone

This cruise *Ranger* was trying out something new. We had aboard some drone missiles that were, as I understand it, modified Super Bee Target drones. The normal use of these drones is to simulate a supersonic aircraft for fighter pilots to practice shooting down high-speed aircraft. Wilily little things that are hard to shoot down. In any event *Ranger* had some aboard. Their mission was to fly into NVA territory and do reconnaissance and return with the goods. I guess if they get shot down, at least we didn't lose a pilot.

The drones were controlled from a shelter (room) that was installed on the sponson forward on the starboard side. No photos were allowed. I was interested in looking into that room but couldn't get close, secret stuff, need to know clearance. Just nosey but then you guessed that. I know nothing of the type of missions.

One day I watched an F4 go supersonic as a chase plane for the recon missile that was being launched from a special launcher on the flight deck just forward of the island on the starboard side. This launcher was only brought up and strapped down to the flight deck when they were going to launch the missile. If all went well, on returning it would deploy a parachute and was snagged in midair by a helicopter...sometimes. Other times they fished it out of the ocean...it deployed a floatation device. Anyway, an F4 would 'chase' it into Vietnam. The missile would launch just as the F4 closed over the ship at better than Mach 1. As I was on my way up to UHF-1 I noticed they were going to launch the missile so I stopped on the ladder to watch and then I looked aft and saw the F4 closing on the ship, really getting in gear, impressive in full afterburner when it is hitting its pace. I was halfway up the ladder on the outside starboard side of the island when the missile went off. I was impressed, it went off the launcher in a blink and the sonic boom of the F4 passing to port almost knocked me off the ladder even though I was on the starboard side of the island. Glad I was holding on.

As a side note, on the hangar deck there was a very nice suite of advanced test equipment built into a long rolling trailer assembly, something like 12 feet long. The missile would be rolled up next to it for evaluation. Of course, I remember the test set, very impressive collection of electronic test gear. No photos were allowed

Later in life I had a very good friend in the Silicon Valley, Jerry Lawson, who had worked for the company, I believe it was Kaiser Electronics, that supplied the test gear. Jerry had designed and built that test suite setup! We had talks about it and he knew all about the test gear and the program. Small world, huh! Jerry had also been a 'Tech Rep' for the big rotating radar used on the E2 Hawkeye. Jerry was a notable engineer in the history of the Silicon Valley, San Francisco Bay Area, later becoming a video game pioneer at Fairchild. There is a school in Los Angles named for him.

The Day the Dial Fell Off

Sometime in early 1970, Yankee Station, Gulf of Tonkin. My primary duty in USS *Ranger* was the maintenance of the computer data link communications equipment for NTDS and later, IOIC, Integrated Operations Intelligence Center. There were four primary data links in *Ranger*. Included in the "maintenance" duties were some operational duties. I was personally responsible for changing the codes in the encryption equipment for NTDS Link-11. I will not go into detail about how this equipment operates, you will know why when you finish reading this. Link-11 was an encrypted high-speed digital data communications link with other NTDS ships and aircraft, namely the E-2 Hawkeye, to exchange tactical data, radar contacts, commands, etc. The code in the encryption equipment was changed each night at midnight.

The process was to personally take the plugboard, the daily code was set into a plugboard, to Radio Central, meet with the communications officer, sit in front of him and plug the new code into the plugboard. Put the plugboard back into the black bag, black of course, for the walk back to the computer room where the equipment was located. At Midnight I would open the safe door of one KG-22 and change the plugboard. Both KG-22 encryption equipments were located inside separate safes. In a few minutes the data link was back on the air and after confirming the data was good from other ships, I would repeat the process for the backup KG-22. I was usually in bed by 1AM and would be up at 6AM.

In order to be the "Quick Draw McGraw", first ship to be back online after the code change at midnight, I usually took the plugboard out of the backup KG-22 around 11PM and changed the code in it so the switchover would go in seconds. If the primary KG-22 failed during that hour it would only take a minute to swap plugboards with the backup and be back online. They never failed.

Duke was the only other person approved to change the code, so Duke and I shared this duty.

So, one night at 11PM either I or Duke spun the dial on the backup KG-22 safe and the dial fell off onto the floor. Now we are down to one KG-22. That night we were a little slow getting the link back online, but no "Quick Draw" on subsequent nights.

In the morning I had the ships locksmith come up and take a look at it, he had a secret clearance. I asked if he could open it and he said he could and would get his equipment. When he returned with big tools and a torch, I said whoa! I asked if he could just put the dial back on and he said he could, but it would surely be in the wrong place and the combination would not work. I told him I thought he would bring some listening equipment to get the thing open...he said I watch too many movies. We were at sea and the whole ship was making noise to say nothing of the equipment in that room, so I don't know what I was thinking. This equipment was located in the computer room which was a classified space but not a 'secret crypto' space, that is why they were in safes.

I dismissed the locksmith with a thank you. I could not let the safe be damaged, if I did we may have to have a Marine guard on the safe 24-7 for the rest of the cruise or until it was somehow repaired. I could just see requesting that.

There is one thing to know about "Crypto" equipment in the navy...it does not belong to the navy. It belongs to the NSA, National Security Agency or "No Such Agency". The NSA has strict, very strict, extremely strict, death could be part of it or maybe just the part where you wish you were, rules about their equipment. A good part of Crypto School was learning just how strict and all the things you need to do to safeguard their equipment. The first clue to the seriousness of the school is the instructors wearing side arms, the second clue is when you find out the maintenance manuals are printed on phosphors paper, except for the Red Covers. No smoking around these manuals, if a flame touches the manual there will not be enough dust left to blow off the table. It is quite a problem because if that were to happen who would know if it all went up in smoke...they have an answer for that...don't ask. When I used the manuals, which was not often, I would clear the room except for two witnesses who watched from the other side of the room, I don't smoke and I was always careful where I placed them. The manuals were kept in a big safe in the secure communications area of Radio I and when I checked them in or out every page had to be counted in front of the communications officer.

I was the only person trained on the KG-22 in USS *Ranger* at the time (another person would be trained later). Duke was my backup person for help in changing the code, always have a backup, he had a TS crypto clearance like mine but was not allowed to maintain the equipment. I was the only person authorized to do any work on the KG-22's and was directly responsible to the NSA, that part was about to become very apparent.

So, there I was at sea level with the dial in my hand, as the story goes. I knew I was not going to 'blow' the safe and I was not going to set up a cot next to it and have my meals brought in for God only knows how long to get an authorized group, if any existed, to actually replace this. It would not be easy.

I decided to have a look at the mechanism inside the safe door, so I opened the one working safe for a look. There is a small window in the safe door to allow the error indicators to be seen during normal operation. In looking at the inside of the door it looked like if the window was removed then, maybe, with a small slip pliers I could remove one nut and the entire mechanism would fall out and the door would open. A lot of ifs.

I got the locksmith back up for a chat. He pointed out that the glass I was talking about breaking, about 3" by 4", was 24 layers of safety plate or impossible to break and I would also run the possibility of breaking the window mounts (welded and screwed) before the glass would break.

In anticipation of breaking the glass, I actually thought it would be easy and was confident the nut would turn, I went to the Radar Switchboard Room to make my own window. The Radar Switchboard Room was one of our equipment spaces where we had a little hobby shop of sorts where some of the guys made trinkets and crafts out of acrylic, Plexiglas. I made a replacement window from clear Plexiglas. As I was putting the finishing touches on my new window, I noticed we had an engraving tool there on the bench. I decided to sign my name on all four of the newly sanded edges of the window. The signatures would not be visible from any angle when installed. Just a lark but at least I could identify it as my window.

I decided to take a chance and told the locksmith to bring up a "star" bit (chisel) and a 10-pound sledge. We started in to break the glass but could not even crack the first layer. He said he had a bigger hammer, a 20-pound sledge, as I recall, maybe it was bigger. It took a while but we finally did break through, amazingly, without damage to the mounts or anything else. I was in luck; the nut was loose and I spun it off by hand. The mechanism fell out of place, just as I expected, and the safe was open. The locksmith repaired the lock, I replaced the window with my Plexiglas one and reassembled the safe mechanism and we were back in business. The CIC Commander was happy, the Electronics Material Officer was happy, and I was happy, "all's well that ends well", right. Just a normal day's work as a navy DS.

I ordered another glass window through normal supply channels and wrote a report to the NSA explaining everything I had done but I left out the part where I signed the edge of the Plexiglas window. I guess when you write a report to the NSA that you modified their equipment in a "field expedient" manner, it sets off bells, apparently big BELLS, to say the least.

Now with 50 years of retrospect, I think I should have known better. Guess I'm just a slow learner. It is not like I wasn't told.

A month or so later into the deployment in the Tonkin Gulf *Ranger* made port in Subic Bay, Philippines for the usual nine days of refitting and R&R before returning to the combat zone.

In port the Electronics Material Officer, LCDR Woodward, called me to the EMO office. I reported to the office to find LCDR Woodward and two civilians, they looked like the trouble type; I mean who wears a suit coat in the Philippines. We rarely see civilians in the EMO office. They informed me that I was being placed under arrest for violation of the national secrets act by possibly compromising NSA equipment in a war zone, during the war! They had a new glass window with them. I thought "you guys didn't have to 'hand deliver' the new window". I guessed they wouldn't think that was funny. Their claim is that anyone could have used a soldering iron to cut through the Plexiglas and open the safe, compromise the unit, and replace the Plexiglas without anyone being the wiser. I guess this was possible, even though it was in a classified almost always occupied space.

My ass was saved by the engraved signature on the sides of the Plexiglas, the information that was not included in the report as a matter of secrecy, so I explained to them. After much conversation and inspection they were satisfied the equipment could not have been and was not compromised and left with their handcuffs and bulging suit coats. It did not occur to me to ask how they enjoyed their flight to the Philippines.

A supply channel request for a new glass window for a crypto safe and the report I wrote really sounded an alarm. As I recall we never did receive a new glass window through normal supply channels, I guess the NSA really does know all!

Back On-line Tonkin Gulf

Sometime in early 1970 LCDR Woodward called me to the EMO office and told me there was a problem with the SRC-16 in the USS *Sterett*, DLG-31, a Guided Missile Frigate operating on South SAR, (Sea Air Rescue) just off the southern coast of North Vietnam. I was to round up the usual sea bag of parts, Helo over, and fix it. Flying to another aircraft carrier is one thing but flying over to a DLG and landing on their small Helo pad was exciting, I felt like a celebrity.

By the time I got there they already had one channel, of four, working, great guys. I helped repair two more channels and showed them how to repair the TGC module. I had to stay overnight; it was fine. The only thing I didn't like was the galley was only open at mealtime and you had to get there fast or not eat. Unlike the *Ranger* where the galley is open 23 and a half hours a day for anything you want. If you happen to want what they're serving, usually good.

The North Vietnamese navy has a bad habit of tying a high-speed motor torpedo boat to a 'Junk' and sailing it out close to ships operating just offshore...like South SAR. Then when the time is right zooming to attack the ships.

I learned all this when the ship suddenly went to General Quarters (Battle Stations). Of course, I didn't have a GQ station being a visitor, so I stayed with one of the DS's in CIC where we happen to be at the time.

What happen was the operator of the digital sonar picked up high speed screws, the telltale sign of a fast motor torpedo boat in the water and sounded GQ. The *Sterett* turned away from the threat and went to flank speed, really got in gear. The Fletcher Class Destroyer, all metal and lots of 5" guns, that was running with us turned toward the target and began an attack. Fletcher Class DD's are hell on motor torpedo boats, they can have 20 radar directed 5" rounds in the air before the first one gets to the target and for the most part they will all be on target...this is not WWII.

The next day the Helo picked me up and back to *Ranger*.

The youngest Petty Officer First Class in the Seventh Fleet

Shortly after I was informed that I made DS1 LCDR Woodward called me in and said my presence was requested at an awards ceremony on the Fo'c'sle. I arrived and was told to stand in the first line but still had no idea what 'award' I was to receive, certainly none that I knew of. The Commander pinned some medals on some and then called me out as the youngest First-Class Petty Officer in the Seventh Fleet according to Bureau of Naval Personnel records. Congratulations! Four years and five months from age 17 at that time. That is certainly not a record for first class but maybe from age 17 at the time. Four years and eight months officially by date of rank. The navy average to make first class at the time was 9-11 years.

In WWII my dad made MoMM1, Motor Machinist Mate just before he turned 19 and that probably wasn't a record, back then if you could do the job you went up in rank fast. I learned early, the 'doers' get recognized, sooner or later, and the 'slackers' will complain the rest of their lives that they can't get a break.

More Shore Patrol and 'Cinderella Liberty'

'Cinderella Liberty' means everyone back on base by midnight. Yet another day and night of Shore Patrol in Olongapo City. Olongapo City, for all intents and purposes, was one long main street lined with bars and here and there a curio shop or a restaurant, in the broadest sense, and some 'short time' hotels. It should be noted that Olongapo City does not represent the best of Filipino culture any more than Tijuana in the notorious days represented the culture of Mexico. That being said few sailors will talk much about Olongapo mostly because you would not believe a word they said. In those days it was sin city.

The main street started right out the main gate of Subic Bay Naval Station, across a small bridge over a drainage canal very close to the gate. Pardon my French but the canal was referred to as "Shit River". The gate was guarded by well-armed marines. Across the bridge was like the bad parts of the old west brought up to date, it was the first time I saw people walking the streets with Thompson sub-machine guns and sawed-off shotguns! Of course, they were some sort of armed security. Then there was the 'PC', Philippine Constabulary, sort of the State Police but dressed in army type BDU's, Battle Dress Uniforms, and always armed, of course. Then there were the actual police, again armed and tough as they come. Pretty much every one of the above was on the take and there were few rules. One rule was keep the sailors safe.

It was said the Chinese Mafia ran the entire city and so if a sailor was to get hurt and the navy was to shut the gates they would lose big money each day.

All this was to make sure no one bothered a sailor! It was relatively safe for the military personnel to just relax and have fun, of course if you got drunk and 'gave' all your money to a young lady...they couldn't save you from that.

Aside from the SP Headquarters just inside the main gate, the Shore Patrol was divided into seven sectors or 'Beats' starting with Beat one at the bridge and Beat seven at the Market Place, as it was called, plenty of bars. Beat seven was considered the most dangerous Beat, sort of the edge of civilization. Civilization being on the other side. I am not sure how many miles it was out to Beat seven, but it was miles of bars all the way.

Every bar had a live band and plenty of girls. There were bars that catered to certain groups, for example, only Blacks. Another example is guys from a certain division on the ship, I know many of the electronics guys frequented certain bars. Of course, there was nothing violent about it, anyone could go anywhere. People just gravitated to certain places they liked and the girls and the bands. There were incidences of the girls getting into fights over a guy...jealousy...Butterfly knives and all! If you sat with a certain girl in a bar once it is best that you looked for her the next time you went into that bar or there could be trouble. I am sure many guys had a "best girl" in more than a few bars. Apparently that was OK.

The girls were mostly young and beautiful, I guess they had to be to compete. There were girls from the farm that were earning money to support their impoverished families, there were some with a first-rate education as well, most looking for a better life. I know of several good marriages from there. Like anything it comes down to choices.

Mostly shore patrol duty was pleasant enough, go into a bar and several girls immediately come over and want to invite you to come back the next day when you are not on duty. Offer photos, so you can know them when you return. Bands, dancing, floor shows, guys getting drunk and having a great time and doing things they would never do in front of their parents. Not many fights to break up or anything like that. Sailors don't want to end the night in a shore patrol brig so most of the time they stay in line...until they get too drunk. There is always a few that become 'Superman' after one beer. Their buddies and the girls are good at keeping them in line.

One year every bar in Olongapo City had a live band playing a very good rendition of the Beatles 'Hey Jude'.

A Night on Beat 7

Being on Shore Patrol so many times, I am sure I had all the beats more than once. I was in more bars than anyone that makes a concerted effort to cruise all the bars. The most dangerous was probably Beat 7. As a PO1 this time, I was the Beat commander, I had about 10 or 12 Shore Patrol including myself. We always patrolled in pairs, so that would be five or six patrols for beat seven. I tried to swing past the police station often to make sure I was up to date with anything that might be happening on the Beat. We carried night sticks but otherwise were not armed. The Hard Hats, the permanent shore patrol were armed. Not much reason to be armed, the local security takes care of everything.

On Beat 7 in a bar that was upstairs on the second floor, my partner and I observed two suspected sailors in civilian clothes. Civilian clothes were not allowed unless you were attached to the base or you were an officer. I needed to verify their identity. They were sitting with two very young girls; one girl was standing on the table and had her dress over one guy's head. I just had to interrupt that to check Id's, of course. They both refused to show their ID's, I insisted, then they said they were officers. They still needed to prove it to me. Right at that time the bouncer came over and threatened to throw me down the stairs if I didn't get out! My partner stepped back toward the stairs a little, SOP so he can get help if things go bad. I told the bouncer in no uncertain terms the bar would be off-limits forever if he didn't back off, he noticed my partner ready to go. He backed off. Now I insisted on seeing the ID's or I would place them under arrest! This time I guess they knew I wasn't joking...they were officers off a Destroyer. The last thing they needed was to be arrested by the shore patrol. I won't go into everything else that went on there; I am already at risk of not being believed! But in the interest of full disclosure, no farm animals were involved...that I observed.

I stopped to check in at the Police station and the police had a Filipino civilian suspect in custody, I do not know what he did but they were going to question him about something. I never did hear the questions, would have been in Tagalog anyway, but I didn't stick around after they threw him against a wall and started beating on him. Some pre-questioning understanding and attention getting. I had no say in anything the police might do if there was no sailor involved. They would never have done that to a US Military person. Not to say that you can't break the law there, you certainly can and one thing for sure you don't want to go to a Philippine prison!

Philippine prisons do not have food. If you are imprisoned you better have friends and family. The US Embassy makes a daily run with food for the US citizens that are incarcerated.

Just another day on Beat 7.

Incident on the Bridge

On one of the nights I was on Beat 7 it was getting close to midnight and we were closing bars and 'backing out' everyone. There were Jeepneys and other vehicles taking guys back toward the base, bar operators were coming out into the street to let us know if there was anyone passed out in a bar. The owners knew they had to close and not to let anyone be left behind. We cleared Beat 7 and were transported to Beat 2 or 3 to continue herding guys toward the base when I heard a fast eight shots ring out followed by the distinctive 'ring' of the clip being ejected from an M1 Garand! We were just close enough to hear the clip eject. I knew that distinctive sound well. I actually did not count the shots but know the M1 holds a clip of eight rounds. Couldn't imagine what was going on. When we heard the shots, we were keeping down because it sounded close. My friend Sven was on the bridge at the time, he was shore patrol on beat 1 or 2 that night and was, by that time, at the bridge keeping guys moving. Sven told me that a Filipino man stole something from a sailor and ran down to the canal, jumped into a boat and made a run for it when he was shot by the PC. I remembered thinking there was one person in the boat. I was told that a boy swam out to the boat and returned it to shore where a bloodied wallet and watch were returned to the sailor who was quite sober by then! I understand the marines were none too happy about it. Anytime shots are fired around a marine they run toward the firing, guns in hand! Sort of a habit.

Recently I called my friend Sven, we kept in touch from time to time over the years and asked him if he remembered the incident, I was sure about my memory, who could forget. Sven wrote the following to me:

> "Yeah, I remember the incident. Actually there were two in the little boat with a motor. Some people were yelling something and a PC (Philippine Constabulary) soldier got out of his chair by a money exchange near the bridge and walked out onto the bridge. Actually I believe this was a drainage canal, not a river. As he walked onto the bridge he took his gun off his shoulder, pushed someone aside, aimed and in the automatic mode, emptied his gun into the boat. The bodies slumped into the boat and water as the boat kept running along. The soldier then put a fresh clip into the gun and walked back to his post by the money exchange. I don't know what happened with the boat since I was busy with some other SPs and a Marine from the gate, trying to keep sailors and Marines off the bridge. As I said, I was busy after the shooting with trying to keep the bridge clear of looky-loos to see what happened to the boat and its occupants.

"The Great Beauty Book" or "Call of the Sirens"

Back out at sea. Time for lunch. I head down to the second deck to the medical department. *Ranger* has a full two ward hospital with five doctors. I was a little early to meet my favorite medical corpsman, HM-2 Tom Clemans, for lunch. Tom had the duty today as the 'Pekker Checker', we were at sea nine days out of Subic and the VD line was in full swing. Tom told me we had 500 cases of the CLAPP (Gonorrhea) this time. Usually all the cases that are going to show will show within about nine days. The price one pays for answering the "Call of the Sirens".

Since I was early Tom told me to take a seat for a few minutes, he was just finishing up. I noticed two large scrapbooks on the table and started to look through them. Both books jammed with portraits of very gorgeous young girls. I asked Tom what this was all about. He told me that guys in the VD line were encouraged to look through the book while waiting in line and see if their girl was in there, if not then just add her photo. Wow, I guess stay away from the cute ones!

All the ladies in the profession were required to carry a medical card that was supposedly validated once a week after an examination. I guess a lot can happen in a week, right?

Social Advice

In one port of call in Subic an ET-2 on his first cruise approached me in the compartment and asked me what to do to stay out of the CLAPP line. I recommended staying on the ship or on the base! He said he wanted a girlfriend, I guess he had enough of hanging with the guys out at sea. In any event I would be the last person to ask for social advice.

Someone else said to go out the first day and find a girl he thought he would like and buy her out of the bar for the whole nine days we are in port. Then bring her on base and have a good time, base clubs, Grande Island Resort (a navy resort island where everything is free, beer, food, and nice beaches), movies, etc. Sailors were allowed to bring female guests to Grande Island. There is also Olongapo City. The point is to occupy full time. Anyway, you get the picture. If you make a lucky selection, then you can skip the CLAPP line! If you want to play Peter Rabbit, good luck. He mentioned later this is exactly what he did and had a terrific time with his new girlfriend. He was all smiles nine days out of port and still able to pee!

Today all this seems very crude, but it was the time, the time before HIV, AIDS and worse. Even then most of us resisted the 'Call of the Sirens'.

Supervising the SPN-10 Group

The AN/SPN-10 is a complex system for landing aircraft automatically in any weather. It is the first operational system of its type and was developed in the late 50's. It had limitations. The SPN-10 had two radars to track two incoming aircraft at the same time, a vacuum tube analog computer, accelerometers fore and aft on the ship, and two large display consoles located in CATAC, the Carrier Air Traffic Control Center. Information from the system was fed to digital converters and then to the NTDS computers and data to Link-4A for communications with our A6 Intruder, A7 Corsair II, and F4J aircraft to allow full or partial control of the aircraft for automatic landing and other tactical purposes. Each aircraft has a 'corner reflector' that is usually lowered with the landing gear. This reflector is tuned to provide a bright reflection at the exact radar frequency of the SPN-10 radar for very precise tracking of that particular aircraft type.

On aircraft carriers' aircraft do not 'take off' and 'land' they are 'launched' and 'recovered' (or 'trapped'). This is somewhat tricky; the aircraft being recovered needs to adjust its speed so that the flight deck is pitching down at the time it reaches the deck to 'trap' onboard and hook the 'wire,' one of four cables across the flight deck the aircraft tail hook must catch. The SPN-10 has accelerometers to constantly measure the pitch and yaw of the flight deck and feed this information ultimately to the aircraft autopilot to adjust the speed and position of the incoming aircraft. Just one of many things going on here.

Due to the nature of vacuum tube analog computers, drift and so on, it was deemed to be risky to actually bring an aircraft all the way to the deck. The operational modes were:

Mode 1 – full computer control of the aircraft via data link 4-A interfaced to the aircraft autopilot all the way to the flight deck. This had been done in tests but not in *Ranger* that I know of.

Mode 1A - full computer control of the aircraft via data link 4-A interfaced to the aircraft autopilot until ½ mile, 10 seconds to trap, then the pilot takes control. By this time the aircraft is lined up and speed adjusted.

Mode 2 – Data link information is sent to the aircraft but the pilot sees it on a display and manually flies the plane. Known as 'flying the needles'.

Mode 3 – The air controller watches the console display and talks to the pilot on the radio.

I don't pretend to know everything about landing the aircraft on the carrier, somewhere in all this the LSO or Landing Signal Officer, also known as 'Paddles', has control over this and there are flight deck lights of all sorts, center line strobe lights, Fresnel lens light bank known as 'The Ball' as in "Call the ball", "Roger ball" from Top Gun, that changes color if you drift off the glide path.

The SPN-10 group lost the ET-1 that was in charge of the group. LCDR Woodward asked me to look in on the group, officer talk for you are now in charge of that as well as everything else you have until we get someone else. As I recall they had four ET's that were assigned to the group. That is a lot for a shipboard system but keeping it running and aligned was a challenge. I did my usual asking the tech's a lot of questions, tried to build a little "esprit de corps" with some slight organizational changes. That worked out and people were happy, probably happy I was leaving them alone. In this role I was mostly a go-between to LCDR Woodward. In any event things were going well and the gear was well maintained. It was a short assignment. I never worked on the equipment, I didn't really know enough, and the ET's were good.

I held tours and answered questions from pilots. Several pilots wanted to know all about the equipment that could be flying their plane automatically.

One of my questions to the techs was, what if we have to recover an aircraft in Mode 1, what do we need to do and how can we check the alignment of the system to make sure it is safe? I was horrified to find that in order to verify the alignment of the system we need to erect a couple 20-foot poles with a corner reflector out at the aft end of the flight deck! Imagine doing that with 30 knots of wind coming down the deck. This is impractical and impossible if the need were to suddenly arise. Bad weather, zero zero visibility and have to bring a plane onboard would be risky. A 50's design, analog computer, vacuum tubes. Drift in the circuits that had to be corrected all too periodically! Just part of the maintenance task for this system.

My concern was the ability to satisfactorily use the system in Mode 1 if it were really needed. Even for Mode 1A it would be good to have some sort of check on the alignment.

Design of the Portable ACLS Receiver

I noticed the SPN-10 consoles in CATTC (Carrier Air Traffic Control Center) had a grey box on top of the console with aircraft cross needle type indicators. A new grey box that was not there in Cruise 7. When I found out this was monitoring the actual RF data link from Link-4A to the aircraft I had an idea. One day in port I took one apart and found it contained a data link transceiver, control head and indicator, I recognized it as used in the F4J.

AN/SPN-10 Display Console #2 in CATCC, Photo from *Ranger* 68-69 Cruise book
The grey box on top the SPN-10 console is circled

I sketched an idea for a box containing the same components with a 28VDC input connector that could be carried in the Plane Guard helicopter. The Plane Guard is the helicopter that is always in the air when launching or recovering aircraft. The idea was to be able to do a quick alignment check of the SPN-10 when necessary while under way. It was simple, the helicopter pilot would put the unit on the dash and switch it on then fly the 'needles' and observe the 'Ball' at the same time as an alignment check for the type of aircraft that would be recovered. Different aircraft had different glide slopes.

LCDR Woodward told me to go ahead and build one. I had the aviation sheet metal shop make a box and I got the radio and other parts from supply and wired it together. I initially designed it to fit between the seats next to the pilot but after the first flight the pilot said he got vertigo trying to use it. So I turned the indicator 90 degrees and said put it on the dash when in use, otherwise store it between the seats. That worked.

Received some recognition for that effort. The first 'on the fly' alignment check for the SPN-10 system. No photo of it, somehow we just didn't take enough photos back then.

By 1970 on the east coast the new AN/SPN-42 all digital ACLS system was being evaluated by the navy to replace the aging SPN-10 so many of these problems went away, the future marches on.

Button, button who has the button, this button isn't working

On good days the air traffic controllers would generally have three or more aircraft in the approach pattern, as one trapped aboard one more went into the pattern. The SPN-10 could track only two aircraft on approach at a time. It had two radars that each 'locked on' to two respective aircraft and two consoles to control them from. As one aircraft trapped aboard that radar would automatically break and go out to catch the second aircraft after the next one on approach in a 1, 2, 1, 2 arrangement. The controllers used the SPN-10 to track the aircraft in the approach but as an aircraft got close to the ship they wanted to break the track without waiting for the aircraft to actually trap onboard and go after the next track to bring the 1, 2, 1, 2 action a little faster. Aircraft carriers are a target when they must stay on the same course recovering aircraft, so move it along in high gear. *Ranger* had the best air traffic controllers. I knew some of them, they were hot!

One day I received a complaint that a button on the SPN-10 console was intermittent. I went to take a look so I could confirm the nature of the problem then I would send someone that actually knew the equipment to work on it. My idea of Public Relations.

The controller said the button that allows the radar to disengage and go out after the next aircraft was intermittent. I looked at the button in question on the console and saw that it was a lighted pushbutton just like the rest but had no function label on the panel. I didn't think much about it because the button was by itself low on the short panel under the main display as I recall.

In any event I got one of the guys and told him we need to check this button out. He took me aside and said they have trouble reports on this button on both consoles all the time. I said maybe it is about time we got it fixed. Then he told me the 'rest of the story' that the button was only hooked up to 24VDC to illuminate the button and that actually the button had no function whatever beyond pacifying the air traffic controllers!

Apparently in the past controllers wanted some way to make the radar break track when they know the aircraft is in the slot and go out to the next aircraft even though the SPN-10 does this automatically when the aircraft traps onboard. The ET's drilled a hole in the console, very professional, and installed a lighted push-button that looked just like the rest.

Every time they get a complaint they go look at it and proclaim it is fixed! Then everyone is happy until the next time a controller gets aggravated. There was actually no way to make it work. The best kept secret in the ship. ET's aim to please.

The Young Filipino Man on the Bus

It was around early April or May 1970, *Ranger* was in Subic, I took five days leave and went to Cavite to Carolina's parents' home for a visit. To get there I had to ride on the Rabbit Liner, a really decrepit old bus. The type of bus you see in the old movies, chickens in cages inside the bus, hot, etc. The bus had a roof rack, I remember thinking these chickens should be outside. I didn't think that anymore when we were driving through the jungle. It was very interesting, when the bus went through a village it would slow down entering the village, open the doors and let some kids on the bus then slow at the other end of town and let them off. They were selling sodas and some things to eat including Baluts. A Baluts is a partially developed duck egg made by burying the egg in warm sand until it is ripe! I was the only Caucasian on the bus. The nice-looking young lady sitting next to me bought a Balut and when she removed the top of the shell and bit the furry head off the duckling I knew then I was not interested in having one. I had a coke.

I was near the front of the bus, away from the chickens, and in the seat in front of me was a smartly dressed young Filipino man. The bus went in and out of small villages and somehow in the middle of nowhere the engine stopped. I thought 'this is just what I need', I knew there were communist guerrillas in this general area of Luzon, stopping is not recommended.

The engine was mounted alongside the driver under a cover, yes inside the bus, the driver opened the cover and tried a couple times to get it going. He clearly didn't know what he was doing. The well-dressed young man started talking to the bus driver and the driver stepped aside and the young man fussed with the engine and had it going again shortly. I thought 'he is going to get that white suit dirty' but he didn't. We were on our way again. We started talking and I learned he was 24 and a shipyard worker at Subic, a machinist. I laughingly told him he should be in the navy.

I checked my old notebook, yes, I still have it, trying to find his name. I found the entry I wrote at that time, Joe Palma. Now I remember I probably became more interested because his last name was my wife's family name but no relation. Joe related to me that he wanted to join the navy, it was his biggest dream and that he had submitted papers but the navy recruiter in Manila wanted money under the table and that he and his family were saving up! This really bothered the hell out of me! I got his work address at Subic and said we will meet when we both get back. I told him 'get all your paperwork together'. Five days later I was back in Subic and he invited me to his house in Olongapo. His mother and sister were there too. I reviewed the paperwork and it looked to me to be in order, I took it with me and said I would return the next day.

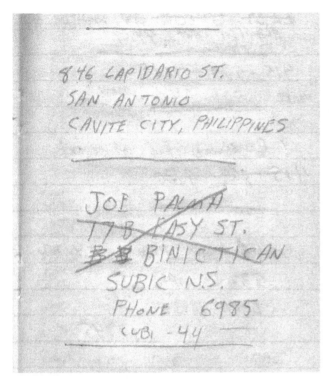

846 LAPIDARIO ST.
SAN ANTONIO
CAVITE CITY, PHILIPPINES

JOE PALMA
77 EASY ST.
BINICTICAN
SUBIC N.S.
PHONE 6985
CUBI -44

Joe's phone at Subic written in my book right below the address of the house I was visiting in Cavite. Crossed out when Joe sent a letter from Boot Camp

Being close to the Filipino community and many of the Filipino sailors in the ship I had many times heard the stories of families paying navy recruiters 'under the table' for their son to join the navy. At the time the Philippines was a prime recruiting ground for the US Navy and had been since a few years after the Spanish American War when the Philippines first came under US control. Carolina's father was one of those recruited in 1912.

I took the matter to the JAG in *Ranger*. The JAG told me that he couldn't do anything about it directly but that I could go to Manila with a letter from the JAG inquiring into the situation. He said they probably know we don't have power but if you start with the chief saying that you have a letter of inquiry and request to see the commanding officer, you will probably get what you want before you ever get to see the commanding officer. Sounds like a plan to me.

I flew on orders to Manila from NAS Cubi Point next to Subic Bay with the letter in my pocket. The aircraft, by the way, was the best looking, neat as a pin, all white and polished, pristine 1940's US Navy DC-3. Yes, a DC-3, saw many as a kid but now I finally got to ride in one. The navy really took care of this one.

I was a brand-new DS1 and was getting used to, let's say, not getting any arguments. Almost as good as being a chief (CPO). I went into the recruiting office in Manila and, as it happens, a senior chief came right over to me. I said I was there inquiring about an applicant to the US Navy, 'maybe some sort of problem with his enlistment, I have a letter of inquiry from the JAG'. He looked at John's papers that I had with me and asked me what I wanted. I said certain persons wanted to know if there is a problem with his enlistment since he is an outstanding young man that has garnered the attention of certain brass. Then I mentioned again that I have a letter of inquiry from the JAG and should I wait to see the commanding officer over this. The chief assured me this would be handled now, sent someone to get Joe's actual file, I saw it, he looked at it, said he didn't see a problem and handed it to a PO2 saying, in front of me, process this guy in...get him in here ASAP. I wrote the chiefs name on the back of the letter and said, "This should satisfy the inquiry, I know the JAG will follow up as routine". Left in time to catch that beautiful DC-3 from Sangley Point back to Cubi and *Ranger*. No one ever read the letter.

I guess, now, 50 years later it seems like a gutsy thing to do for something I had no stake in, but I was a bit of a hard charger and I didn't like what was going on. I guess the old chief knew that for whatever reason he didn't want a 'kid' PO1 (I was just 22) to start anyone looking under the covers at the recruiting station.

Joe wrote me from boot camp about a month later, I corresponded with him a couple times and then lost touch as I was transferred off *Ranger* and on to Dam Neck, VA.

Maybe I should say a little more about this. I was starting to be known for not being afraid to stir the pot when it came to someone bending Naval Regulations. In this case I was close friends with many Filipino sailors in *Ranger* and often heard their families paid for the privilege. That had always bothered me. I already guessed that a DS1 with only one hash mark, ships patch, and three rows of ribbons, signs of a 'salty sea dog', and looked all of 18 would likely be perceived as a 'bad go getter' so I purposely wore my dress white long uniform that shows the one hash mark, each hash mark indicates four years' service. The average time to make PO1 in the Navy at the time was 9 to 11 years, it would not be the first or last time I attracted attention for being a so young PO1. The JAG was right that any recruiting office with the reputation they had for years was likely 'walking on eggshells' and if they really were crooked I would get what I needed and never see the commanding officer. Anyway I was legally inquiring into the matter. Nothing to lose, and it was fun. OK, I was nervous but I didn't let it show.

Many years later I did hear the recruiting office in Manila had a scandal, surprise, surprise.

The Owl

If any of our aircraft sustained battle damage or any serious problem on a mission over Vietnam, with few exceptions, they would be mid-air refueled and 'bingo' into the airfield at Da Nang for repairs before returning to the ship. We normally did not attempt to bring battle damaged aircraft back to the ship when there was an alternative. I did once see an A6 Intruder come back aboard with a large hole right in the center outboard of one wing.

On one such mission a *Ranger* F4J was bingo to Da Nang and sat on the tarmac for a couple days being repaired. Routinely the nose cone, which hinges open revealing the AN/AUG-10 fire control radar dish and other electronics, was opened and probably remained that way for some time there. An owl flew into the nose electronics area and rested behind the radar dish. Consequently the repairs were completed and the nose cone and other doors secured and the Phantom flew back to *Ranger*. What a ride for the owl! I always wanted a ride in an F4J but not perched behind the radar dish.

The aviation guys were having a field day with the owl taking it all over the ship and looking for cockroaches for it to eat, don't know how they made out. I saw the owl personally when someone brought it into CIC shortly after its arrival. It smelled like hell! I don't know what eventually happened to it, I bet it didn't last long.

USS *Brinkley Bass* DD-887, Callsign **ADJUSTER**, USS *Camden* AOE-2
USS *Ranger* CVA-61, Callsign **GRAY EAGLE**
taking on fuel, ammunition, and spare parts
Yankee Station, Tonkin Gulf, 1970

In Subic Again, Met Eli Ring, Scotty, USS *Chicago*

After another of many line periods *Ranger* was docking at the Carrier Pier at NAS Cubi Point, Subic Bay Naval Station, our usual place. I spotted the USS *Chicago*, Guided Missile Cruiser docked on the Subic side across the bay. I knew my friend Eli Ring was assigned to the *Chicago*. As soon as I could I left the ship and went to the *Chicago* for a visit.

After a quick tour of the *Chicago* Ring and I went out to Olongapo and had a beer or two in a quiet bar there, mid-day, no band or floor show yet, nice to catch up. I knew that Scotty had also been assigned to the *Chicago* and asked Ring about him. Was he working out? Ring said, "Scotty sweeps the floors", said they couldn't let him near the equipment. I kind of expected that, I had worked with him in the labs in school. He was very bright in the classroom though, thought that might count for something but guess not. If your hand doesn't fit a screwdriver it will probably fit a broom...with practice and concentration.

Eli Ring

I want to say more about Eli. We became fast friends in the barracks at Great Lakes going to ET School, Eli was a couple months behind me. I went DS and he also went DS, then I went to Mare Island for 'C' school and he also went there. We had a great time especially at Mare Island.

There were three pool tables in barracks 930, our barracks. One day we went into the pool room and a guy was there making some good shots and bragging to everyone how he was on the 'Pool' team at his college. Have you ever heard of such a thing? I could see that really impressed Ring, yea right. Ring was a short and unassuming guy but was actually about five years older than me but looked like a kid with the blond hair and all. Anyway Ring asked the guy for a game and he agreed right after he finished the current game. Ring told him to break and he didn't get anything on the break. Ring proceeded to run five tables in a row calling every shot then just said thanks for the game and we moved on to the ping pong tables. Mouths were dropping the whole time. Ring was teaching me to play ping pong. Ring was good at ping pong too, he and another friend, Toline, went to the Ninth naval District Ping Pong Championships, placed second in the doubles. All I can say is there must have been some really great players there.

At Mare Island I was in the top bunk and Ring was in the lower bunk. I learned that real smokers reach for their cigarettes simultaneously with swinging their feet out of bed in the morning and without opening their eyes! I never smoked cigarettes but you learn these things in the navy.

On one particularly interesting adventure back at Great Lakes during ET School Ring and I were at Galley 409 waiting in line for chow on a really cold and gloomy Saturday, no school. Ring noticed this guy in front of us was reading a chess book and he said to him "I see you are reading so and so's book". The guy, in a very superior manner, said "yes, I find it somewhat interesting, do you play"? Ring said yes maybe we can have a game. It was decided that after chow he would come to our barracks for a game, Ring asked him to bring his chess board. When the guy got to the barracks he saw there were four others sitting there with chess boards set up. He was upset and said he thought they would have a one on one game, Ring assured him that he would have a serious one on one if Ring lost. The guy agreed. With five opponents and boards set up Ring went to the window turning his back on the players and played five simultaneous games calling every move, never looking at any of the boards, checkmate on each one!

Turns out Ring had an 1800 ranking in chess, just below Master. His father was a US Navy Captain and I think Eli had a somewhat easy life probably until his father found out he was otherwise occupied in college. Fathers are like that. Ring said he had a couple years of college and told me once he never wasted any of it studying! Caught up with Eli many years later, he stayed in and made chief. I am sure one of the great ones.

The Marine

The Marine Detachment in *Ranger*, also referred to as 'MarDet', was a very well-respected unit. The MarDet had a separate compartment on the third deck that was off-limits to anyone except a marine. They kept their weapons in the compartment with them and were always ready for any emergency. There were at least two exits from their compartment. Some of the duties included providing security detail for the admiral, the captain, the executive officer, and other senior officers. They also ran the Brig, (shipboard jail), and they guarded the special weapons magazine.

The MarDet adopted a foster child in Hong Kong named Li Lai Ha in 1965. Every year when *Ranger* stopped in Hong Kong they would have a big party for her. In 1970 she was 13 years old according to the cruise book.

The marines were well respected...and not to be messed with.

The MarDet party for their adopted foster child Li Lai Ha   Photo from *Ranger* Cruisebook 1969-1970

Early 1970 found me on shore patrol again in Subic, a new DS1. This time I was assigned to the shore patrol main station just inside the gate. As a First-Class Petty Officer I was the lead at the station except for the 'Hard Hats', the permanent shore patrol was the ultimate authority. The 'Hard Hats' were called that because they wore helmets to distinguish them from the temporary shore patrol like me.

If someone passed out in a bar, sadly often enough, the bar operator would go out in the street and flag the shore patrol to come and get him. They didn't want any trouble.

The Hard Hats arrived back at the main station with an unconscious marine in the van. I had two guys take him out and lay him on the floor so we could check him out. I recognized him as a *Ranger* marine. He was alive and I quickly determined that he didn't need medical attention, just another drunk, so to speak. I started going through his pockets while my PO2 wrote down the contents on a report on the clipboard. When I got to his top shirt pocket I found drugs, 'Reds', 'Uppers', etc. Now I knew what his problem was, more than just drunk. I bagged them separately and told the PO2 not to write it down for now.

I called the MarDet in *Ranger* and spoke to the gunnery sergeant. I told him I had an unconscious marine from the MarDet and he had drugs on him. He asked me if I charged him and I said that I did not and he could send someone to get him. Basically saying "he is all yours". The gunny's voice sort of told me this guy was a troublemaker but I was going to let the gunny sort it out.

Soon a van arrived from the *Ranger* with two marines, they tossed the guy in the van and I handed them the report of contents that did not show the drugs, the bag of the contents of his pockets and the bag of drugs and they left. Like it never even happen.

Frankly, a sailor may have been in real trouble here but I decided to let the marines take care of their own. Probably not my call but I called it anyway.

In the ship out at sea when a group of prisoners from the Brig are being moved from one place to another the group forms up in a single line 'chest to back' with a marine armed with night stick in the back of the line. The first guy in the line shouts "make way, prisoner" as the 'snake' moves through the ship every leg in unison.

A couple weeks out at sea I was on the second deck going to chow when I heard "make way, prisoner" coming my way, I stepped aside and at the front was my marine looking like he was recovering from rough handling, may have been the seven mile van ride to *Ranger* from the shore patrol headquarters, but who knows.

What is worse than being a marine in a marine Brig? Off hand, nothing comes to mind.

The MIG

A quick discourse on RADAR in the fleet on Yankee Station, Gulf of Tonkin 1969-1970. *Ranger* had two powerful air and surface search radar's, the SPS-37, a 230MHz low frequency radar with an antenna that looked like a set of bedsprings and the SPS-30, very high frequency radar, and with 6 Million Watts of power, was reputed to be the most powerful air search radar on ships. These were integrated into the NTDS computer systems. Also radars from other ships were sending contact information over Link-11 to everyone's computers. Included in that would be contact information from the E-2 Hawkeye with a powerful radar that looks down on everything. No one gets through!

Most radars are not perfect, the SPS-30 often paints a faint video on the PPI scope that may not be easily observed by the operator. The SPS-37 paints a fat video on the scope, the operators like to use it for that reason. The typical radar antenna of that time has what are called 'lobes' which are vertical areas where the signal strength is strong however these lobes do not always overlap causing blind zones where an aircraft might not be detected.

Now the MiG. This MiG was flying straight for us, we picked him up on the SPS-30 but could not see him on the SPS-37, strange. Then it became obvious that he probably had a radar receiver in the plane and was guiding toward the ship in the radar antenna blind zone. Without a special receiver to tell you to go high or low this could not be done. He was seen on the 30 radar and was reported on NTDS from other ships, what he was trying was impossible. He was fooling one radar out of many. The two F4J Phantoms on BARCAP, Combat Air Patrol over the fleet, were dispatched to investigate. We saw him coming a long way off, enough time to dispatch a helicopter to the area fifty miles from the ship. We never let anything get closer than 50 miles to the ship without an escort. That was the range of the Russian air to surface version of the Styx missile. NTDS ID'd the target as a 'Hostile', the Phantoms ID'd the target as an NVA MiG. Several of us were in the far corner of CIC gathered around IC3, an NTDS console routinely not in use. We watched as the CIC commander gave the Phantoms the 'Green Light'. The first Phantom put a Sparrow III in the MiG and the second Phantom got the big piece with a Sidewinder. The pilot ejected and was floating down in a parachute as the helicopter circled him. He went into the water and two Combat Swimmers jumped in from the helicopter. They rescued him but he was already dead.

The rest of the story is this. My good friend HM-2 Tom Clemans, in the medical department, and I were at lunch and I mentioned the dead MiG pilot and wondered how he died. Tom told me he took cyanide and had no papers or ID of any kind, no dog tags, and no unit markings on the uniform, nothing. I guess dead men really don't tell tales. Not even their nationality.

Going into Cambodia (May 1, 1970)

It was a very large operation when the US went into Cambodia on May 1, 1970. In *Ranger* we had been building bombs for days. The bombs were even on the mess decks, two 500 pounders to a cart, little yellow carts tied down. The tables were all retracted and stored. When you went to eat you could sit on a bomb which is not dangerous, just balance your tray with one hand, fork in the other. Some would take chalk along to write messages on the bombs, usually crude messages. Not being very artistic, I left the chalk in the computer room. While sitting on a set of 500 pounders I was reading the nomenclature on the bomb, MK...whatever and the date of manufacture, we were still working on the 1943 bombs! These bombs were made in 1943. Back in the day they were probably headed for Japan but weren't needed.

I recalled the trucks with covered loads that were passing my high school in 1964 and wondered if those were the 42' bombs or were they 43' too?

Communications were locked down during this time. I remember Ed Buselt said he would have liked to have sent a message to his stockbroker. I often wondered what that message would have said.

I was thinking of Jerry. I knew he often flew up near the Cambodian border and figured he was in the thick of it. Found out later that he was very much in the thick of it.

When the day came for the invasion *Ranger* started flying what are referred to as 'Turnaround Alpha Strikes' which means 'send every plane that can fly' and when they return refuel and rearm and get back in there, repeat as many times as necessary.

Take them for their shots

I hated shots more than anything. Lots of guys were evading getting their shots. Right after I made first class ETCM Joyner came to me with a list of 22 men that were due for shots and my name was on the list too. He ordered me to get every one of them together and get down to sick bay and see that everyone got caught up on shots. I did and as the senior ranking guy I had to go first, damn, four shots, at least they were all in the arms. I had to brave it out in front of everyone. Funny thing is, haven't had a problem with needles since.

The Dentist

Ranger had a crew of between 4800 and 5300 (we sailed with 5300 in Oct 69) and five dentists. The dentists were actually there for the pilots. It turns out that breathing oxygen and maneuvering at high speed and high G stresses in a jet fighter requires healthy teeth. The crew gets in after the pilots...as it should be.

One day a young dentist, I had to check Cruise Book 9 to be sure, Lt. Graves came knocking on the computer room door wanting to know if anyone could repair his little Hi-Fi set he had in his stateroom. I guess the ET shop sent him over because I repaired the one in the admirals' stateroom, ET's are a jealous lot. Anyway I repaired it. Then he said he should do something for me. How about thousands of dollars in dental work? I did need a tooth filled so I went down for that. It should have been my first indication, for a week after the filling if I touched that tooth with a metal object, like a fork, I would get an electric shock. That finally died down just before the Hong Kong visit and, of course, I hadn't learned my lesson, I went back for more. He said I should have my wisdom teeth out. There was nothing wrong with them but they 'might' cause problems in the future. I foolishly made an appointment with the 'Wisdom Tooth King'.

Lt. Graves asked which side to do first and do the other side later. I asked which is easier.

He said the right side was growing out some but he would have to cut into the left side. Slow learner, I should have run right then. I chose the easy side, no cutting for me right now. Short story short...it was miserable, there was nothing easy about it. In addition I had not realized the constant vibration of the ship would not allow the pain killers to let me sleep or even sit up.

Never went back. I still have the wisdom teeth on the other side, never experienced any problems. Lt. Graves was a very good Dentist actually and always had a great smile, funny guy.

Hong Kong 1970

The annual visit to Hong Kong, the third one for me. Good times, I liked to walk around and visit the shops. Everything was cheap. $6HK to one-dollar US. I bought some more Hi Fi equipment, in years earlier I bought a sewing machine for home. Hong Kong is also the finest place to eat! I loved going to upscale restaurants, the service was great. One time I left the ship and went into town just for a crabmeat cocktail, great.

Many of the guys were touring the many bars of the Wan Chai district. This is where I collected on my shore patrol duties, no shore patrol in Hong Kong for me. Can't tell you anything about the bars in Hong Kong.

The Chinese Young Lady

One of our DS's, call him DS2 Van, as he related to me, goes into a bar and finds a very nice young lady and hits it off pretty well with her. He mentioned she seemed very inexperienced at being a bar girl. Anyway he makes a deal with the bar owner to take the girl out of the bar for the rest of the week we would be in port. This was not unheard of. She could speak no English. Apparently, they had a great time and went swimming, movies, parks, etc.

Soon enough the week was up. Van had the duty the last day in port and couldn't get out of it as he had earlier. So she was returned to the bar and he went back to the ship, he was pretty sure he explained things carefully and that she understood.

That last day in HK I also had the duty. I answered the phone in the computer room, it was the chief on the 'After Brow', where the Ferry boat pulls up. As always *Ranger* was anchored out in the bay. The chief asked if we had a Van there, I said we did, he was sitting right in the computer room, what is the problem?

"The problem is that we have a young lady here that wants to get in the ship to see DS2 Van...and she has her suitcase with her! Better get down here now (the polite version)"! I said we would be right down. Van and I went down and she was there with everything she owned and was giving the chief a hard time. She was refusing to leave.

She was a relatively plain looking very young woman who seems to have not progressed to 'bar girl' makeup yet. Not a typical 'experienced' bar girl type that we would often see. Seemed to be very innocent.

I signed her in and we headed for ET shop 2, couldn't take her to the computer room. Fortunately we had an ET that spoke perfect Chinese, Frank from SF, wouldn't you know. Frank talked to her some and explained to us that she was raised on a "Junk" with other children in her family. They were very poor; she didn't step on dry land until she was 16 and didn't go to school. She said her father recently sold her to the bar, not an unusual sad story. She could not believe that we had no women in the ship. She looked around almost comically and wanted to show how she could clean things up for us. Everyone was enjoying her visit. Van and the guys took her down to chow and then showed her around the ship. She could not believe it was so big. She really wanted to stay. She would have had no arguments from the ET's, they are not always good at keeping the shop clean. Anyway, no voting.

I told Van to keep everything in the open. I was sure there was not going to be anything untoward happening but I wanted to make it very clear. At the end of the day I escorted them down and signed her out so she could leave. She was crying but finally convinced that she could not stay. Sad case and very unusual. One thing, she didn't seem to get that we were a combat ship, didn't seem to know what military is, as if we were a supply ship of some sort and we all dressed alike.

The Slob

Murk Krum, one of those times when the name says all you need to know. One of the things you can do onboard ship to earn the ire of your fellow shipmates is to be a slob. Neatness and cleanliness are important when living in such close quarters.

DS2 Krum was a special case, he was very short of common sense and wasn't a very good technician either. He was already a DS2 when he came onboard *Ranger* or he would never have been recommended for promotion. He would sleep in his uniform which is prohibited by navy regulations. He failed to send dirty clothes to the laundry, if he wasn't already wearing them, and he also wasn't sending his bedding to the laundry either. He was told and ordered many times to clean up his act but failed to pay much heed to that. He wasn't arrogant or stubborn about it he just had something missing. Finally when his sheets were actually black some of the guys threw them away. This would normally be a time when you get new ones and explain what happened to the originals, etc. But for Krum, he barely notices and began sleeping on the mattress without the cover and sheets and in his work clothes.

Krum was a DS but we had no use for him and he was assigned to the ET shop, tool issue group, taking care of test equipment. The ET's are a tough bunch in many ways and I am sure he was even less appreciated there. In any event Krum was not one of my guys.

At some point, and as a PO1 I was not made aware of this in advance, some of the guys were fed up and when Krum came into the compartment one night, the lights were out even the red lights, in the dark a blanket was thrown over his head and a belt tightened around arms and all. In the navy this is what is referred to as a 'Blanket Party'. He was carried into the head and thrown into the shower and the hot water was turned on and he was, as the story goes, liberally beaten with several scrub brushes by several persons. If you have never been in the shower on and aircraft carrier where the hot water can be very hot you are missing a great show. He was abandoned in the shower.

All this did not seem to have a lasting effect. As I recall he remained a problem.

The rest of the Wells Story

I already spoke of ABH1 Wells, my crooked Company Commander in boot camp. Fast forward to my third year in USS *Ranger*, onboard with me and 5000 or so other sailors, guess what? I spot ABH1 Wells, newly assigned, he reported on with the Air Wing. And still a first class! It is around November 1969; I was a fast moving DS2 at the time hoping to make DS1 in record time. I thought to myself if I make first class I will make sure I see him, meanwhile I will avoid him, easy to do since we do not work in any of the same areas. As luck would have it, I made DS1 on 1 June 1970, date of rank, but was promoted well before that, made first increment, 4 years and 5 months to PO1 from age 17, almost a record. I went looking for Wells…just to say hi. I bumped into him in a short passageway between decks and stopped him to chat. I was a little disappointed because he just made chief, damn, anyway I said that I was in one of his boot camp companies back in 65. He was all smiles... then I asked him if he ever figured out who the broken piece was assigned to. Right away he remembered, just got a frown and walked on. It was great, he deserved to be reminded.

The Jones Incident

In the computer room we had two or three 4 drawer file cabinets that were not in use for anything official and were generally assigned to individuals for personal use. There were no locks on the drawers. I never used one, preferring to keep any personal items in my locker back in the crew berthing compartment.

When the person that oversaw assigning the drawers was transferred, I found myself in charge of assigning the drawers. I didn't mind, not really an official duty.

DS3 Jones was transferred to *Ranger* in time for Cruise 9, he was a 'Display Tech' and was not assigned to my group. Jones was black, now called Afro-American. It appeared to not be any sort of problem in OE division or, for that matter, anywhere in *Ranger* that I knew of at the time. I tended not to pay much attention to the color of a man's skin or his heritage and I think no one else did either. I got along well with Jones and it appeared that he got along well with everyone. We talked several times. He mentioned he was from New Jersey and had experienced some racism growing up. I remember thinking that was too bad but 'well that is over now', this is the navy, probably because of my upbringing. The other thing about my upbringing and the navy was strict adherence to the rules. In the navy rules are rules period. Sailors are sailors, nice guys are nice guys. Color and race should not and as far as I was concerned did not have anything to do with anything.

After some months into the deployment DS3 Jones managed to get in with the wrong type of people. As it turns out we had some blacks in *Ranger* that were organizing a Black Panther agenda of sorts. Troublemakers. Race relations were becoming an issue in the navy about this time in early 1970.

In a subsequent incident in port in Alameda this group held a meeting in the forward mess deck in which they refused a direct order to disband and, as if that is not enough to end any idea of a career, the leaders threatened the OOD (Officer of the Day) always accompanied by an armed marine. With a very short phone call in minutes the room filled with armed marines, the leaders were arrested and put in the Brig, so I heard, I wasn't there. But I get ahead of myself.

As I have said before I am not and was not a racist and I fully expected everyone else to be the same, white or black or brown. Racism from either direction is wrong, I don't owe anyone anything because someone is black or brown and they don't owe me anything because I am white. I thought the navy was going to have problems, and I was right, when they started having separate rules for blacks. We were all sailors in the same navy, rules are rules. Sailors are sailors.

Back to the story. Someone who had a file cabinet drawer was transferred and I had a list of persons that were interested in having one, DS3 Jones was next on the list. I called him in and asked if he was still interested, he said he was, and I assigned it to him.

Within a week Jones came to me and said he was missing some cigarettes from his drawer. I checked into it and discovered the person that had that drawer before Jones always brought lots of cigarettes and made them available free to anyone that wanted them, cigarettes were $1.50 a carton out at sea. I notified Jones of this and suggested that he put his name in the name holder on the drawer, he said he would. I also notified several guys that the drawer had a new owner.

The next day someone asked me if I noticed the name on the drawer, I went to take a look. It was a 'Black Hand' symbol, not a name. I called Jones in again and told him that was inappropriate, and he needed to put his name on it, and now, or lose the drawer. He put his name on it.

It was a shipboard rule that everyone must be clean shaven unless you had an approved medical reason not to shave and there were a few, they carried a card. The main reason for this is that it is very difficult to impossible to seal an OBA (Oxygen Breathing Apparatus, used in firefighting) to your face when you have a beard. It was a safety issue. And a rule.

DS3 Jones, probably with the wrong advice, decided not to shave. The new disobedience, I guess. Since Jones was in the Display group and not under my direct supervision I did not say anything. As a DS1 I could have interfered, but I let it go. In no time the MAA (master at Arms, shipboard police) was throwing him out of the chow line on occasion. Mostly he was still eating. They should have escorted him back for a shave on orders, but they didn't, another one of the rules not enforced for blacks. He was also tossed from the pay line and had to 'let it ride'.

Then one fine day I was working on a project at the workbench in the Radar Switchboard Room and left to go to chow. On returning my project was on the floor and there was DS3 Jones with his feet up on the workbench with a correspondence course in his lap. I was surprised. I asked him to put my items back on the workbench and go back to work. "If he didn't have anything to do, I would find something".

He refused the request, I ordered him to do it, and he refused that too. So, I went to the computer room and asked DS1 Ed Buselt to accompany me to the Radar Switchboard Room. I then ordered DS3 Jones to replace the items on the workbench, he refused a lawful order from a superior petty officer, enough for big trouble. I then ordered him to go back to the compartment and shave and report back to me clean shaven, this surprised him, but he again refused the order in front of witnesses. I picked up the phone and called the MAA and told them I was putting DS3 Jones on report for disobeying direct orders from a superior petty officer. They said, "Bring him down to the MAA office", I said come up and get him, I wanted him placed under arrest. They did and took him away. I expected Jones and everyone to play by the same rules.

I can only guess Jones wanted to be arrested, I obliged. Wrong time and place to be an activist.

In no time at all ETCM Joyner, not only master chief, and a chief when I was born, but now Chief of the Boat (the most senior chief) called me in for a private 'come to Jesus' meeting. He wanted me to drop the charges, said it was bad for race relations. I explained my position. Chief Joyner said he was going to pull the chit if I didn't. I said if he did that I would put him on report too! The conversation ended and nothing else was said. We were soon to be on our way home to Alameda at this point.

I was brushing up on my expected conduct when I would take DS3 Jones before the Captain.

This was never to happen; the entire affair was delayed.

CHAPTER 15

Back at Alameda 1 June 1970

My official date of rank as a DS1 was also 1 June 1970 but I was wearing it for months already, I made the first increment for promotion. Very nice homecoming all around. Another long cruise over. I was looking at a fourth cruise to start in October 1970 but didn't know I would not be on that one.

After the new captain and new EMO and I found out I was being transferred, I happen to meet DS3 Jones in the parking lot near the ship. He happily told me the navy offered him a 'for the good of the Navy' discharge and he took it. One does not have to live long to regret that decision. It is not an 'Honorable Discharge', just you are out like it never happen. Oh, well. The navy is not for everyone, especially if you allow yourself to be talked into an activist political agenda. Choices, choices, you can have a fine career or you can be an 'activist'.

Dump Those Sea Bags or Where Did You Get That Jet Engine

Back at NAS Alameda since I was now a PO1 there were new duties. I was assigned the 'Brow Watch' as assistant to the JOOD (Junior Officer of the Deck), a chief petty officer. The first time in *Ranger* that I stood watch wearing a sidearm. One bright and sunny day I drew duty with a chief that I had not met before but had heard of him. I can't remember his name but he seemed to think that anyone that was getting out of His Navy was someone to be carefully scrutinized! The 'Brow Watch', the gangway, controlled access to the ship checking all personnel other than officers on and off the ship, the usual security, ID cards and Liberty Passes, cursory checks of bags. But when the chief saw that someone was getting out of the navy, leaving the ship with their 'Sea Bag' for the last time, he would often order them to empty the sea bag right there on the aircraft elevator for inspection and sort through everything. If he found any contraband that sailor was in trouble and put on 'legal hold', not getting out of the navy that day! Even a pair of pliers would do it…better be prepared to prove they are yours. Innocent until proven guilty, what's that?

So one day I am there with the chief, why me, and this sailor is leaving the ship for the last time, getting out of the navy, looked a little too happy for the chief. If he managed to get off ship and NAS Alameda he would be out of the navy! But the chief told him to empty his sea bag right there on the aircraft elevator! He had the usual stuff but one interesting thing more, a small component of a J-79 jet engine!

The chief put him on 'legal hold' and he could not leave the ship. An investigation was started, I was not part of that, of course. It turned out he had a complete J-79 jet engine at his house, except for that one part! The F4 Phantom jet fighter has two J-79 jet engines.

The navy agreed to let him off the hook providing he did three things. One, return the engine, they took it from his house. Two, tell them how he got it off the ship, and three, what did he intend to do with it? As far as I know he was not prosecuted.

His story was that as a jet mechanic working in the Jet Shop he would volunteer to stick around and work while in port when most others went ashore. At night he would take parts along with the trash out to the dumpster on the pier and then retrieve them later, been doing it for years. "One piece at a time", the old Johnny Cash song. He said he intended to build a land speed racer to race at the salt flats.

Never have any contraband in your sea bag, especially on the day you are getting out!

The Indian Chief

Ranger docked at NAS Alameda, I have the Brow Watch again, it is late, and probably the midnight to 4 AM watch. This time the chief is a Native American. I had no idea that he was a Native American until he told me, I don't know these things. There is not much activity in the late night so we had time to talk. Right from the beginning of the watch he started in accusing me of being racist against Native Americans. As he continued to goad me and I continued to tell him he was full of it, I began to wonder what this was all about. At the time I actually didn't connect it to anything but later I wondered if Master Chief Joiner had put him up to it. Maybe I was the talk of the chief's quarters because of the Jones incident. I guess it is not every day that someone threatens to put the Chief of the Boat on report.

At the time I was not connecting the dots, he almost had me convinced that I was racist against Native Americans! But I made it through the watch without losing it. I remember wondering "what is this guy's problem". Wondered how he could have made it that many years in the navy with that attitude. Looking back I am sure he was trying to tag me as a racist, I could have saved him the trouble. That would be hard to do because I had a Filipina wife.

Painting the Mast, *Ranger* in Dry Dock

When *Ranger* returned to Alameda we went into dry dock at Hunters Point and at some point I went on leave for a couple weeks. When I got back on a Monday Master Chief

Joiner called me in and told me to relieve ETN-2 Hill who was currently in charge of getting the mast painted. He had a crew of 20 or so guys and had been at it for two weeks and still not done. We painted the entire mast in three days in Subic once with half that many guys. The chief said he wanted it done and inspected by Friday.

The job of painting the mast always falls to the electronics technicians because we are the only ones who know what not to paint and what type of paint to use on the various antennas. Electronic components such as radar antennas, for that matter, any antennas can have their performance reduced by using the wrong paint.

I went up to takeover. Hill showed me what had been done so far, during this process of showing me the progress we climbed all the way to the top of the mast. The 'Crow's Nest', the TACAN Dome (TACAN antenna) is located there...173 feet above the waterline! There is a ladder welded to the mast that leads all the way up, the 'Crow's Nest' is a basket about six feet in diameter, three or four guys could sit in it...if you can find that many guys with the guts to go up there. I was very apprehensive about the whole thing. How could the mast be swaying when the ship was dry-docked, not even in the water! But I was a PO1 and could show no fear...right! As I recall now the second hardest thing I ever did was get off the ladder and onto the 'Crow's Nest' swaying 173 feet in the air. The hardest thing I did was to get back on the ladder, it took me 15 minutes to get my composure enough to get back on the ladder. Hill was used to it and it didn't seem to bother him. I guess the mast wasn't really swaying that much but it was moving and I was looking straight across at the tall buildings in San Francisco.

From the top of the mast to below the yard arms had already been painted so no more visits to the TACAN dome. It was my policy to not order anyone to do what I would not do. I got everyone together and gave my speech. "Everyone will work until the job is done. We have until Friday, but I want it completed by Wednesday". Then I found out that some of my men were from OI Division and were not anxious to be released because they would be put on something else, maybe worse. I told everyone I have them until Friday and if we finish early I will muster them in every morning and then send them home! One issue was the yard arms were not painted and I told everyone that I was not going to order anyone to crawl out to the end and paint their way back. I was not willing to order anyone to do something I was not willing to do. If I didn't get any volunteers, I would request the shipyard schedule the painting which would mean we will definitely be there until Friday. I got two volunteers. The mast painting was finished the next day and inspected Wednesday morning and I sent everyone home...except me.

Friday, I was sitting in the computer room when one of our warrant officers came in and asked me about the mast. I said it was finished and inspected and passed, job complete, I didn't mention that was Wednesday's news. He asked where some of my guys were and I said I relieved them for the day. He was somewhat upset and said I did not have the authority to relieve them early, so I didn't mention that I had been 'relieving' them for the last three days. I stayed on duty the entire time, of course.

Backseat Ride in an F4

In my temporary position with the AN/SPN-10 group I encountered, from time to time, several pilots who wanted to know more about the Automatic Carrier Landing System. The ET's that actually knew the equipment very well were not much interested in public relations with a bunch of pilots. I was happy to give small tours of the equipment, methods, and operation of the ACLS equipment and answer questions. The pilots were interested in the gear and probably wondering if they could trust it. Had lots of questions about reliability. Understandably after the F4J flap control issue some pilots wanted additional reassurances regarding the equipment.

I got along well with one of the pilots and posed the question if I could get a ride in the backseat of his F4J. He said sure! I was very anxious but upon looking into it more I would have to be ejection seat qualified to ride from the *Ranger* on a CAT shot. So it was arranged that he would take me up from the airstrip at NAS Alameda on a Saturday after *Ranger* returned.

At this time *Ranger* was off the coast of California near San Diego on what we referred to as 'duty flight deck'. It was a training time for various aircraft from different squadrons to practice carrier landings. We did this every summer for a couple weeks.

The 'arresting gear' consists of a big hydraulic machine that is just under the flight deck and the cable that is across the flight deck (four machines, four cables) referred to as a 'wire'. The LSO or Landing Signal Officer is in communications with each of the 'arresting gear' machine rooms and tells them what aircraft is going to be recovered next. The weight of the aircraft has to be carefully entered into the machine to provide the correct pull on the 'wire' for the weight of the aircraft. This is critical and is said and acknowledged by each arresting gear operator with an operator on the LSO platform. If the tail hook of a light aircraft caught a 'wire' that was set for a heavy aircraft there would be serious damage and vice versa. It has to be just right.

As *Ranger* was performing the duty flight deck many and varied types of aircraft were being recovered and launched off again. An A4 Skyhawk, one of the lightest aircraft, was recovered. Next in line was an RA5C Vigilante, one of the heaviest aircraft. For whatever reason the number one 'wire' was still set for the A4. The pilot of the Vigilante was a very senior captain and I heard later was to have been assigned to the Pentagon. He was a very experienced pilot and hooked the number one 'wire', the wire pulled all the way out and snapped but it slowed the aircraft down so much that it could not fly off as it would if it missed the 'wire'. Instead it went off the angle deck, veered left and went in the water. No one got out, two very senior aviators were gone.

Over the next couple days there were many very high-ranking admirals and captains coming and going by helicopter from North Island. A big investigation. Needless to say this very sad incident canceled my back-seat ride! Suddenly everything was 'by the book'.

Smith DS1 gets a call

When we returned to Alameda from Cruise 9, we got a new Captain and a new EMO. LCDR Woodward retired, and Lt. Sellers took over as EMO, he was the oldest lieutenant I ever saw. It further did not surprise me to find out that he and ETCM Joyner were buddies, both Chief Petty Officers in the Korean War. I know Master Chief Joyner probably told him how much of a troublemaker I was because Lt. Sellers never said one word to me and never smiled in my direction. I am sure he had me transferred. Probably considered me a 'threat to good order'. They can do that.

Sometime after the return to Alameda and the change of command I was sitting in the computer room when I get a call, it was the Controller at the Bureau of Naval Personnel asking me where I wanted to go...I was being transferred! What! First I heard of it! With only 11 months left on my enlistment I was not eligible to be transferred off the ship. Normally you must have two years left on your enlistment to rate a transfer, I told him okay, but I would not sign an extension. I chatted with him regarding several possible assignments, I turned down instructor duty at Mare Island, and then was offered Chief of Data Communications, a chief's position (E-7) at FAAWTC Dam Neck, Fleet Anti-Air Warfare Training Center, Dam Neck, VA. All the responsibilities but without the actual promotion. I thought that would be a real plum and anyway I would get to stay home for a change.

Careful what you wish for *"The sea stalks the unwary and relentlessly pursues the careless"*!

CHAPTER 16

Transfer to Dam Neck

The Move to Virginia Beach

After arriving back at Alameda I was finally qualified for base housing as a PO1. I moved the family into the old base housing, a ghetto apartment, and started to settle in. Then the news of the transfer. I remember only being there a couple weeks and it was time to pack up again.

The movers came and packed up everything just like when I was a kid, moving again. Carolina and I along with Rose, and Evelyn, Carolina's teenage sisters that were living with us, drove cross country in the 68 VW Bug.

There was an interesting incident with the moving crew, four Spanish speaking men, who were packing up our household goods. To say that Carolina was fluent in Spanish would be an understatement, she was fluent in five languages to the extent of being qualified as a UN translator. Carolina came to me and said the movers were talking to each other in Spanish and discussing which boxes contained things they wanted and were marking the boxes. I asked her to not say anything in Spanish for now.

When the truck was loaded I had them all come inside, line up and give me their names and show their ID's. I wrote it all down and then Carolina explained to them, in Spanish, that if anything was missing they would be prosecuted and their jobs would be forfeit. Everything got to Dam Neck.

When we arrived in Virginia Beach it did not take long to rent a very nice house at 4624 Crown Point Lane, the good life for a change. It had central air and a garage. What more could you ask for?

Dam Neck and Chief Miller

I reported aboard FAAWTC/FPCA, Fleet Anti-Air Warfare Training Center, Fleet Programming Center Atlantic, Dam Neck, Virginia Beach, Virginia on 5 November 1970. Captain Alwyn Smith Jr., USN was the commanding officer of the base which included the FAAWTC/FPCA installation as well as others. The FAAWTC/FPCA was commanded by Commander C. A. McLellan, USN.

The command structure at FAAWTC consisted of the commander, a lieutenant, a warrant officer or two, a master chief (E-9), Senior Chief Miller (E-8) and a couple regular chief's (E-7), nine first class petty officers (E-6) including me, there were about 240 or so technicians', as far as I know, all DS's. I was the youngest first class and had the least time in my rank of any of the nine at FAAWTC. I began checking in to the various departments at the installation. When checking into the FAAWTC building I was directed to Chief Miller.

I know trouble when I see it coming and Chief Miller was trouble. He called me into his office and asked me to close the door and began telling me I would be assigned to 'tool issue'. The DS1 that was assigned to the data communications group was a friend of the chief but not qualified for the job. I was not happy about that at all and I pointed out to the chief that I was on BUPERS orders to assume charge of the data communications group. He told me he made the decisions there and besides it was a chief's position and I told him he was right...I am the acting chief. He was getting angry, especially after I told him to check with BUPERS and if I didn't get the position "my sea bag was packed" and I was ready for reassignment, "let me know before I finish checking in"! I went home.

The next morning he called me in and said the position was mine and to complete checking in, which I did. That was strike 'one'. I knew there would be trouble. But now I was the new Chief of Data Communications with 22 DS's reporting to me, a step up from the at most four DS's that reported to me in *Ranger*.

I did a little checking on Chief Miller. It seems everyone feared him, I mean up the chain of command as well as down. He was very hard on the men and was personally responsible for the zero re-enlistment rate at the facility. No one stayed in the navy after meeting Chief Miller.

Prior to my arrival the chief had taken a dislike to a lowly third-class petty officer and made sure he never got on the day shift, he had a wife that worked and this was hard on married life. When the guy finally rotated to the day shift Chief Miller had a run-in with him and immediately assigned him back on nights. As the story goes the guy wrote to his mother and she wrote to her congressman and this brought a congressional investigation down on the entire base with emphasis on how Chief Miller ran the watch bill (personnel assignments). The commanding officers had to love that one.

But he didn't stop there, he next took a dislike to a DS1 and, as the story goes, harassed him to no end, finally sending the CID to the guys house on a report of stolen government property. Apparently the guy had rescued some stuff that had been put in the dumpster. The guy had enough and went AWOL to Canada. A first-class petty officer going AWOL...unheard of. The stories go on and on...how the U.S. Navy allowed this man to stay in the navy was beyond me.

Word was he was assigned to Dam Neck after some trouble on the DDG he had previously been stationed on out of Norfolk. It seems that it did not take long before the crew had enough of Chief Miller and someone sent a threatening letter to the commanding officer that if the ship left port with Chief Miller onboard it would not return with him. The CID got involved and finally recommended that they just transfer him...welcome to Dam Neck!

Chief Miller had been in the navy 18 years at that time and I had been in for five years with three plus years of sea duty...I had more sea time than he did, that was my first clue.

I also heard that he was TAD from the Norfolk Naval Hospital but never believed it, although he was probably insane, who knows. No matter what he should never have been allowed near the men. In my tour of duty there I often made that clear to superiors but not to the men of course.

My group consisted of 22 DS2's and DS3's. Our task was equipment maintenance, it was a 24 hour a day operation so I ran three shifts. I always worked days and I had some guys that wanted to work nights so I did not rotate them. One, DS2 Kestner, was in my DS-A school and C school class and a DS3 I knew from the barracks at Mare Island, was a class ahead of me, in fact, in my original DS-A school class that I failed out of, more about him later, can't remember his name.

I had one radio room full of HF and UHF radios for the Link-11, Link-14 and Link-4A operation, one crypto equipment room, an antenna farm on the roof and a 60-foot tower located away from the building for the HF antenna. I also had data terminal equipment down on the first floor with the computers (a giant room with rows of computers). I was told FAAWTC had more computers than anyplace in the navy except the Pentagon.

My third morning at the facility as I pulled into the parking lot, Kestner came running out to meet me and told me that Chief Miller had come in at 3AM and caught one of my guys sleeping behind some equipment in the crypto room. I was glad he told me because I am sometimes slow on my feet and need time to consider, remember Karate Joe. I guessed what the chief was up to. Sure enough he called me into his office, closed the door, just me and him, and proceeded to give me hell about how I ran a slack outfit! He said he was going to punish the guy and I immediately told him he would not! I pointed out there was a chain of command and I expected him to honor that and I would decide on punishment, if any, after looking into the matter. The chief was totally 'pissed', the only word I can think of.

But I didn't stop there, I told the chief that I would need to see his security clearance before he would be allowed into the crypto room again. I was reviewing security procedures and would be changing the combination to the lock on the vault door. Double that totally pissed, red face over freckles to match his red hair and all. He was on fire, I thought he would suffer a heart attack, for the good of the navy of course. Chief Miller never produced his security clearance and was not allowed into the crypto space again during my tenure.

I left the office and did not punish anyone in this incident but discouraged taking 'cat' naps in the equipment rooms. I did run a tight group and everyone knew and respected it, I was told. I found that leadership was much more effective by pulling the group together as a team for the mission and cutting out the 'BS'.

Someone told me that my 'reputation proceeded me', I didn't know what that was all about, but guessed there were rumors about *Ranger*. It seems that I was well respected mainly because I stood up to Chief Miller. One of the guys noted that "Chief Miller always had to chew a couple of TUMS after talking to me".

Chief Miller was always looking for ways to make life difficult for me. He just couldn't bring himself to leave me alone and just get on with the navy tasks. His next attempt was to put me in charge of the MDCS task at FAAWTC. This is the 'Maintenance Data Collection System' a mostly paperwork system for collecting and reporting data on equipment failure. This was fleet wide and I had experience with it...but Chief Miller had his own ideas on how it should be done, of course. Involving much more work for me and not being anything like the fleet standard that I knew and was expert on. His excuse was that this was a shore station and not a ship. I wasn't having that and pointed out to him that we had more NTDS equipment than any five ships. It wasn't the MDCS system it was make work for DS1 Smith! A case of 'making up the rules as you go along', can't win.

Over time we had many disagreements and when it came time to write my performance report he did a dandy job of giving me the lowest rating possible and then handed it to me in person. He said I should sign it, as he smirked like the cat that just ate the canary.

Understand that signing your 'Report of Enlisted Performance Evaluation' only indicates that you read it not that you agree with it. Of course I refused to sign it anyway and immediately requested a "Captains Mast". That threw everyone into a tizzy.

The Captains Mast

In the US Navy if you do something criminal the first step before a court martial is the Captains Mast (Article 15 under the UCMJ). A Captains Mast can also be requested to address any issue, but is considered a very serious step, you better be right. In other words "don't bother the Captain" for trivial things...not recommended.

The process after a request for "Captains Mast" is that you will be interviewed, and discouraged to continue, by everyone in the chain of command. This is presumably so they might help you deal with the issue before it gets to the captain. I was first interviewed by the master chief (E-9) who told me it was not a good idea and recommended that I withdraw my request, my opinion of the master chief, no guts, never saw him stand up to Chief Miller, he just let moral slide. Probably working on retirement. Then came the warrant officer, same advice, then the lieutenant, same advice. The lieutenant I recognized from his tenure at the schools command at Mare Island when I was there, pure 'milkweed'.

No effort put forward. It was looking to me like Dam Neck was the place where previously promising careers ended and non-leaders were put to pasture. The whole place was a shock after three years in the combat zone with real leaders of men.

Two days later I was holding morning "quarters", addressing the oncoming and off going shifts, a formation of 150 or so men. A runner came down from the commanders' office and said my immediate presence was required in the commanders' office. I turned the remaining few minutes of holding quarters and dismissing the men over to another first class. This duty was generally rotated among first class petty officers, this just happened to be my day.

At the office of Commander McLellan I was directed by the yeoman to enter, 'they were waiting'. On entering I reported smartly to the commander who was sitting behind his desk. I noticed the warrant officer and the lieutenant were sitting at what looked like attention on the couch off to the side of the office. I noticed one other thing; Commander McLellan had my entire service record open on his desk! I was wondering when someone was finally going to look at my record! Let's see, 4.0 professional performance marks three years in the combat zone, Navy Achievement Medal with 'V', two Letters of Commendation in the combat zone, promoted to DS1 in record time.

Commander McLellan said "I know what you want". I said "Sir, I don't know what you mean", he said "don't screw with me, you want Chief Miller"! I said "yes sir"! He said "you can't have him", he said he will take care of Chief Miller personally. I don't know if I said that he had not done a good job of 'taking care of Chief Miller' so far or maybe I just wanted to say it. In any event he changed my evaluation to something not 4.0 but high enough that I could not take it to the Captain, which would have been my next step. Commander McLellan apologized that he could not make it higher and reiterated that he would take care of Chief Miller. I was dismissed. And, of course, I dropped the request for Mast. Frankly, when a Commander suggests that you do something the only appropriate answer is "Aye Aye Sir".

Two weeks later Chief Miller was pulled out of the chain of command and placed in charge of ... guess what, MDCS with one DS3 to help him. Everyone got the word that Chief Miller gave no more orders. The Commander apparently had enough of Chief Miller too.

My conclusion as I neared the end of my enlistment and my ten months at Dam Neck was that to do the real jobs in the navy I had to be at sea and not see my family much or I had to take the shore duty jobs that were full of 'cast off, milk weed' officers and good for nothing chiefs like Miller. Commander McLellan was great, most officers that rank and above are great and deserve the respect they get. I decided to end my naval career and started looking for a position in civilian life.

It was nice living in Virginia Beach, life was great. Carolina and I rented a very nice house with central air and a garage. I went to Sears and bought a Radial Arm saw and started learning to use it. We bought a dog, a dachshund, named him Wolfgang. Social life was good, had a few parties, that part of life was great.

Had a party at the house once and a couple of the guys were out in the yard feeding my dog Champaign and got him drunk enough to fall over, he was sick, guess even dogs have to learn not to do that. We had something in common after all.

Some interesting things and many good things happened during my assignment at FAAWTC.

Chief Zero

Sometime after I was stationed at FAAWTC, Dam Neck, a new DS1 was assigned to the maintenance group. I didn't get to know him very well. Most of the guys didn't care for him. For one thing he was reassigned to us from a CVA that was in the Mediterranean. It seems he suddenly developed a serious case of claustrophobia which, apparently, no one believed or respected. I guess it just felt like Dam Neck was getting all the mental rejects. Claustrophobia on a submarine maybe but a CVA, come on!

He didn't keep a work schedule that was synchronized with the rest of the routine, claimed that traffic made him too nervous to drive, couldn't risk getting stuck in traffic. That didn't improve anyone's respect for him.

As it turns out he was soon promoted to CPO, DS Chief (E-7). Naturally this did not improve his standing with the men since he already wasn't liked. His duties changed and some thought he was becoming a pain. He now had a desk with a brand-new name block on the desk. One night someone brought in a 'Zero' candy bar and sailors being sailors, trimmed the label and taped it across his name on the desk. It now read "Chief ZERO". In the morning when he came in and saw it he was really upset. One thing you don't do in the navy is show a weakness like that to the guys…just asking for trouble.

The building that housed the FAAWTC was very secure, one entrance, no windows. If the power were to go out it might be dark if the emergency lighting did not work. To guard against this possibility Chief Zero always carried a flashlight. Some thought he was laying it on pretty thick.

In the building we had an electronics shop, a few workbenches, a couple desks, and an enclosed stock room that ran the length of the shop on one side. It had a gate and was usually padlocked. Several people had keys, probably even me. In any event one day Chief Zero goes into the shop to look for some part or other, opens the gate to the stock room, places his flashlight and the keys to one side and enters the stockroom without his trusty flashlight. Several technicians were in the shop at the time, but left…no one knows who but, you guessed it, the last person out quietly locked the gate and switched off the lights on his way out of the shop.

When someone finally returned to the shop, Chief Zero was apparently in some sort of shock, they took him away in an ambulance. Not sure what happened after that, if he got transferred or what. Sailors are cruel sometimes. Apparently even on shore *"the sea stalks the unwary and relentlessly pursues the careless"*.

The Large Screen Display

The mission of the FAAWTC was twofold, one, to train combat information center crews, and the other was to test new fleet computer programs and equipment configurations for the Atlantic Fleet, there was another facility in California for the Pacific Fleet. Throughout the building there were many rooms that were outfitted with all the equipment that would be found in any ship CIC, an aircraft carrier, a guided missile destroyer, a cruiser, etc. There was also an 'aggressor' complex that simulated enemy combat ships and aircraft. The 'aggressor' complex was in a converted theater that still had the big screen. There was a lot of activity around getting a video projection display of the digital NTDS display console information to display on the big screen. They did have a first-generation liquid crystal display projector but it only accepted raster scan NTSC video and the UYA-4 display console did not have such an output. The only real way to get any signal from the console was to tap into the X/Y, and Z signals. A further difficulty was the UYA-4 display consoles had a P-11 phosphor in the CRT's that allowed a pseudo storage function, depending on write current some symbols could 'persist' longer.

The Tektronix sales guy was there and had a Tektronix scan converter, to convert XYZ to raster scan, but the image was breaking up...totally useless. Never mind the timing involved with the 'beam sharing' of the converter, it never would have worked just because of the P-11 phosphor issue. The whole idea was fascinating to me. I was hanging around the edges watching what was going on. Chief Miller came in and when he saw me tried to tell me to move on but then walked away, guess he knew better. Finally when nothing they were trying worked I went up to the officer, not one of ours, that seem to be in charge of the project and told him I knew how to make it work. In truth, I had run back to the office briefly to confirm something in the Tektronix catalog. He was interested. I pointed out the scan converter would never work because it shared the beam between writing the XYZ signals onto the storage media and reading out video from that same storage media. The NTDS console was too fast to allow that and the NTDS display also relied on a P-11 phosphor to retain the image on high intensity writes and let the image fade on low intensity writes. My idea was to buy an inexpensive Tektronix five-inch fine line XYZ monitor special order with the P-11 phosphor and no etched graticule, one of the standard options, and place it into a closed box with a video camera focused on the CRT face. He agreed to try it. I designed and constructed at home a two-transistor level converter to match the UYA-4 console Z output to the Tektronix monitor. I sketched out a box design after checking the focal length of the video camera on hand and the officer had it built. The whole thing worked great. That achievement was another thing that went through the grapevine, everybody heard about it.

Let me add, the Tektronix field sales guy wanted my phone number and later offered me a job. Although I wanted to work there, I declined it when I saw the job application ask what race I was. They did that in those days. I wasn't going to bring my wife into that.

The large screen projector was black and white, nobody had 'color displays' then. The technicians would use a TV tuner to check the large screen projector in the morning by showing Captain Kangaroo. Had to love that!

Meanwhile Back at the Ranch

The *Ranger* was making Cruise 10 without me. As my good friend Sven and I discussed strange things many years later he wrote to me about something that happened in Subic. I just had relate this.

Apparently there was some dredging work on the waterways separating NAS Cubi Point where *Ranger* was docked and Subic Naval Station. A bridge across the canal had been removed not to be confused with the bridge separating Subic from Olongapo City. Sven had made DS1 and was now occasionally assigned to Brow watches. This is what Sven described:

"Did I ever tell you about the horse? We had pulled into Cubi Point and they were doing some work on the drainage system for the swamp. Various bridges along the road that leads around the bay were removed to facilitate dredging efforts. Thus, they were using liberty boats to take us back and forth from the ship to the Fleet Landing. The night before we were to go back to sea, I had the 0000-0400 watch on the sponson that the liberty boats used. I was a 1st class at the time. The last liberty boat had left, and this 3rd class and I were at the top of the sponson talking and killing time. All of a sudden, this sailor, who was soaking wet comes up the ladder from the boat landing area (a small barge tied to the ship). In a slurred voice he says, "Request permission to come aboard, sir." I looked at him and said, "How the hell did you get here?" But thinking that would have been a damn long swim. His reply was, "I rode my horse, sir." I had the 3rd class help him to his berthing compartment. The 3rd class returned shortly, saying that they ran into a buddy of the drunk and he let the buddy have him. A short time later we began to hear noises coming below where the boats would dock. We both went down the ladder and there was this damn horse tied to the landing and treading water. The 3rd class untied the horse, which then swam back to the shore. I made an entry in the log. The next day, some officer looked me up and wanted more information about the horse and who the sailor was. I told him we just thought he was a drunk returning to the ship and didn't think it necessary to take his name. The officer then told me that someone had hired a taxi to bring him back to the ship, after the boats had stopped running. The taxi took him as far as it could go and let him out. This was not far from the riding stable. This guy broke into the stable and saddled up a horse, and used it to get around the dredging works. From some of the muddy horse prints, the sailor got the horse into the water at the little small boat ramp, at the end of the pier and rode the horse to the boat landing alongside of the ship, since the brows of the land side of the pier had already been removed. The horse found its way back to the stables".

One of My Guys

As I mentioned one of my guys was a DS3 that was in my original DS-A school class, the one I failed out of and had to repeat in the next class. I knew him again from the barracks at Mare Island, he was in the data com class ahead of me. I just can't remember his name, let's call him John. After graduation from data com school John was assigned to the USS *Forrestal* CVA-59. As you may know during the first mission launch on Yankee Station in the Gulf of Tonkin on July 29, 1967, there was an accident on the flight deck. This is the accident Senator McCain was involved in, he was one of the pilots in an A4 Skyhawk on the flight deck. The flight deck was loaded with heavily armed aircraft when a rocket from one plane suddenly shot across the flight deck and hit another plane causing many explosions and fires in the worst carrier fire since WWII, with 134 dead and 161 injured. John was a DS3 assigned to the NTDS data communications group. He related to me one day that when the fires started and the bombs started going off he tried to go to the flight deck but stopped to help a wounded pilot that had fallen down the ladder (stairs) from the flight deck. He said the wounded pilot was a mess and it shocked him a little. To shorten the story John ended up assigned to a group of twelve men whose job was to go about the ship and recover bodies of men that were dead and put them into body bags for recovery later.

They performed this gruesome task most of the day and finally came to rest back in the computer room. Shortly a chief poked his head in the door asking about their group and they said they were all in. The chief said there was one more area to check, someone thought there may be bodies there. John, who was not known for his can-do attitude basically was upset at the thought of going out again and let it show. Candidly, almost with tears in his eyes, he told me he had a 'fit' and let it show. The others told him it was Ok, to just stay put they would go out this one last time and take care of things.

The area to explore was the 03 level, Port side passageway, aft. The 03 level is right under the flight deck (flight deck is the 04 level). The 'battery locker' is a room for maintaining lead-acid batteries for use in various vehicles such as aircraft tow and forklift equipment and is located on the 03 level, port side, aft. Lead-acid battery maintenance spaces are never located below the water line, for good reason. It happens that a bomb went off above the battery locker rupturing stored lead-acid batteries and rupturing a large tank of sulfuric acid and blowing the hatch to the passageway open. Saltwater used to fight fires on the flight deck had swirled down into the compartment. Saltwater and sulfuric acid form deadly chlorine gas, odorless and deadly. All of the guys he worked with were killed when they went back there to recover bodies! That and his attitude in general is why John was still a DS3. Until this time three and a half years later he had not recovered from this horrific event. John just didn't seem to care anymore.

Forrestal fire, just getting started, there are bombs on these planes

Forrestal fire, by this time many of the brave Damage Controlmen (DC), the professional firefighters
have already been killed in the earlier explosions

Four months later I was in USS *Ranger* (CVA-61), a *Forrestal* Class carrier, in the same
spot launching our first strike...but no fire.

The hole these guys are looking into would be right at about the 'Battery Locker' compartment
where lead-acid batteries are maintained and drums of Sulfuric acid are stored safely away from sea level

One day John shows up late for work. I asked him why he was late and he related that he had to take his children to the dispensary. John had a wife and two small children and lived off base in a poor neighborhood, no AC and not much of anything else. In those days a PO3 with a wife and two kids would be on poverty row. The doctor told him "his children were suffering from heat prostration and he needed to get an air-conditioner for them" John told me with a smirk like 'how the hell can I do that'.

Sometimes when you are growing up seemingly meaningless little things come back to be important. I was raised in an army family, dad was a Sergeant First Class, and so I grew up in the military and was alert to some of the small things that happen in military families. "You have to take care of your men". My dad took care of his men.

I asked John for the doctor's name, then went to the dispensary and asked the doctor if he told John to get an air-conditioner. He said that he did because John's children were in dire straits in the Virginia summer heat and humidity. I asked him if he would write a prescription for the air-conditioner! He seemed a little confused but then looked at me and said 'sure'. The Doc didn't ask any questions. I knew there was a place on base where furniture was issued for base housing. Now I had a doctor's order for an air-conditioner, I did not plan to mention that the use would be off-base. Back at the FAAWTC I told John we were going to get an air-conditioner and to get his old pickup and meet me in front. We drove to the base housing supply warehouse. There was a PO2 and a PO3 working there, the PO2 was in charge. We went in and I handed the prescription from the doctor to the PO2 and said we needed an air-conditioner, doctor's orders. He seemed a little reluctant at first but wasn't going to question a PO1 or a doctor so he sent John with the PO3 to get the air-conditioner from back in the warehouse. While they were gone I related what John had been through on the *Forrestal* and that his family was not doing well, almost had us both in tears. When John got back with the air-conditioner in the truck the PO2 asked him if he had beds for the kids, he didn't, so a couple beds went on the truck, he asked john if he had a kitchen table, he didn't, so a new dinette set went on the truck. Soon the truck was loaded so much we had to tie it all down. As we left I told John to drive home right away mid-day, it would be easier to get off base. The guys at the warehouse knew the stuff wasn't coming back, no paperwork. Like it never happen! Sometimes things 'never happen' in the navy.

It didn't take long for word to spread to all the regular sailors at FAAWTC that I was one DS1 that took care of his guys. In fairness I am sure not many of my counterparts had my experience growing up.

Admiral Zumwalt and the Shah of Iran

Some more equipment background. In the USS *Ranger* CIC (combat Information Center) we had a very complex and all-encompassing radio receiver known as the AN/WLR-1. Its function was Detection, Classification and Targeting.

When an enemy is searching for you using radar their transmitted signal can be received at a distance greater than their ability to see you on their radar. This is because the signal reflected back to the radar is weak at long distances but the direct transmitted signal is stronger for a longer distance forward.

The AN/WLR-1 could receive and display this signal information allowing the operator to manually process them, measuring the radio frequency, pulse width, and pulse repetition rate of a radar signal. This information was then looked up manually in the "RED" book and that would identify the type of radar and give some information for other signals to look at for further confirmation. One could then determine what type of plane was doing the searching, for example the presence of a certain other emitter could identify a Russian Bear Bomber approaching or a different configuration would ID the incoming target as a Russian Badger bomber.

The WLR-1 would also give the bearing and through NTDS with the bearings from other ships the exact location of a target was known well before they see anything on radar.

The WLR-1 was too manual and slow, getting 'long in the tooth' so to speak and several companies were working on modern replacements including TRW with an example being developed at FAAWTC, Dam Neck. I was very interested in the project even though it had nothing to do with my duties.

I met some of the TRW engineers and got along well with them. I was offered a part-time job after my regular navy duty. I accepted and went to work on project 'Shortstop'.

'Shortstop' had a bank of receivers that could identify any frequency instantly and cross it with the 'Red' book that was now on a hard disk drive. If you so much as keyed a transmitter of any kind it had you.

That brings us to the day when I was assigned to standby, in uniform, at one of the 'Shortstop' consoles during a VIP tour. In a way I was a bit nervous because I didn't know how to operate the console. Fortunately we had operators and I was just window dressing. Although I knew a little about the system I was not briefed on what to say to a visitor.

The VIP visitors turned out to be the Chief of Naval Operations, Admiral Zumwalt, and the Shah of Iran. I was standing by at arm's length of both of them when they came by my station. I didn't feel too bad that I wasn't personally introduced.

At that time Iran was a stabilizing influence in the Middle East and the Shah was buying navy F-14's and NTDS systems for the defense of Iran.

Another new VW Bug

Danny Collins was a DS1 at Dam Neck. He had purchased a new 1971 VW bug. One day in the office he complained that it was too small for his family after all and he wanted to get rid of it and buy a larger car. He had made a down payment and paid on it for about five months as I recall. He said anyone could have it if they just take over the payments. Problem solved, I said "sign me up". Now I had two 'bugs', they would come in handy in the Massachusetts winters to come. I drove them for years.

Our new yellow 71VW and the 68VW

CHAPTER 17

Getting Out, August 1971

I guess I really decided to end my naval career a couple years earlier when I did not extend my enlistment by two more years to 8 years for 'Pro Pay', which was an extra $150 per month, big money at the time for a sailor. I wanted to work in engineering someplace. I submitted an application to Penn State since I was a Pennsylvania Veteran. I also met a recruiter (headhunter) and he lined up five really impressive jobs. I had good advice to go to college and not to look for a job because "if I started to make that kind of money I would not quit". It was good advice that I did not take.

The navy offered to transfer me to NEL, the Naval Electronics Laboratory, San Diego rather than lose me. NEL was where NTDS was invented. I was tempted but after the FAAWTC experience I imagined it would probably be populated with 'Cornstalk Sailors' and I passed on the offer. I had had enough.

I was offered a position at New York Telephone managing a major telephone exchange on Manhattan, this was the highest paying offer I got, and Carolina was fluent in five languages and was looking at the UN to work as an interpreter. There was a new company called MCI that was expanding, they wanted me too, still time to work on telephones, decisions, decisions. Then Digital Equipment Corporation flew me to Maynard, Massachusetts for an interview, airline tickets, rental car, and money, just to come to the interview. Massachusetts is astoundingly beautiful outside the 128 Beltway in late August. At the main plant in Maynard I saw one million square feet of nothing but computers. I was offered a great position as a corporate level Field Service Representative in the International Product Support group. It was heaven for engineer want-to-bees'. I would also be working in engineering as part of my position. They hired Carolina into a great position too when they found out she was the private secretary to the Admiral at Little Creek, VA.

I called Penn State to inquire about my application, they said I can start in the fall class. I asked about my high school grades and SAT score from six years ago, they said six years in the navy, no test, 'you are in the starting class if you want it'.

Slow learner, I took the position at Digital Equipment, no regrets.

The position at DEC was the lowest pay and the greatest job of all my offers, at $9,800 a year, but in those days that bought a good life and a nice house on Lake Boon five miles from the Maynard, MA plant. The starting pay offer for NY Tel. was $18,500, but telephones and NYC, not for me.

The two VW Bugs came in handy in the Massachusetts winters, 10 Wt. oil in the engine, studded snow tires, and take the battery in the house every night. Always got to work.

"The Sea stalks the unwary and relentlessly pursues the careless". Goes for dry land too.

USS *Ranger* CV/CVA-61, callsign **GRAY EAGLE**, remains silent. USS *Ranger* was decommissioned July 10, 1993 at North Island, California as the last crew marched down the gangway. My son Ron, and I were there to witness the ceremony. USS *Ranger* was commissioned in 1957 and I had the honor to serve in this great ship for more than three years of this 36-year history, 1967-1970. USS *Ranger* CVA-61 received ten battle stars on its Vietnam Service Medal. I was there for seven of them.

The USS *Ranger* was scrapped on 1 November 2017 after many years of effort by the USS *Ranger* Foundation to save *Ranger* as a museum. As a side note most of the NTDS Consoles and other Combat Information Center equipment was rescued and is installed in the USS *Midway* CVA-41 museum ship now on display in San Diego, CA. The CVA-41 guys did a great job, very nice display of everything working. It is worth the trip. The *Ranger*'s anchors and anchor chains are now part of the USS Ronald Regan CVN-76.

May you always have 'Fair Winds and Following Seas'

Glossary

1MC, ship wide loudspeaker announcing system

AFB, Air Force Base

AHC, US Army term, 'Assault Helicopter Company'

Agent Orange, a chemical that was sprayed from aircraft to defoliate certain areas of land, for example, along riverbanks to prevent ambush attacks from the river bank

AK-47, Chinese or Russian made assault rifle, selectable full or semi-automatic fire

AWOL, Absent Without Leave

BOQ, Bachelor Officer Quarters, Officer barracks

BoonDockers, ¾ high work boots

Boot Camp, Basic Training or Recruit Training, the first military training

Brig, Navy jail, shipboard jail

C-130, large turbojet four engine transport aircraft

Callsign, special name for a person, installation or ship used in radio communication

CAPT, US Navy commissioned officer rank of Captain, O-6

CAT, steam catapult for launching aircraft, *Ranger* had four catapults

CIC, Combat Information Center, the electronic and command heart of the ship and the task force

CMDR, US Navy commissioned officer rank of Commander, O-5

COD, The utility cargo aircraft used to transport personal and cargo to and from *Ranger*

Corpsman, US Navy Medical Corpsman, enlisted medical personnel, trained for combat medical care

CPO, US Navy enlisted rank Chief Petty Officer E-7, Senior Chief E-8, and Master Chief E-9

BOQ, Bachelor Officers Quarters, officer's barracks

DOD, Department of Defense

DS, Navy Enlisted Rating, Data Systems Technician

EMO, Electronics Material Office or Officer, the EMO is in charge of all the electronics in the ship

ET, Navy Enlisted Rating, Electronics Technician

Ensign, US Navy commissioned officer rank of Ensign, O-1

Galley, naval term for dining place, or chow hall (army)

GQ, General Quarters, shipboard assigned battle station, "go to battle stations"

GRAY EAGLE, radio callsign for USS *Ranger* CVA-61

Homeport, a ships official base of operations

"In Country", refers to being on land (generally in South Vietnam)

IOIC, Integrated Operational Intelligence Center

LDCR, US Navy commissioned officer rank of Lieutenant Commander, O-4

LT, US Navy commissioned officer rank of Lieutenant, O-3

LTJG, US Navy commissioned officer rank of Lieutenant Junior Grade, O-2

LZ, Helicopter Landing Zone, a designated spot large enough to land a helicopter

MAA, Master at Arms, Shipboard police force

Mare Island, US Navy base at Mare Island, California, near Vallejo, California

M-16, US Army standard assault rifle, selectable full or semi-automatic fire, caliber .223

MARS, Military Affiliate Radio System, an organization of Amateur Radio operators with support from the military.

"Milk Runs", easy duty, considered generally not dangerous, all things being relative

NTC, Naval Training Command, separate base where service schools are located

Piece, Recruit Training Command term for a drill rifle, de-milled rifle for drill purposes

PO1, US Navy enlisted rank, Petty Officer First Class, E-6

PO2, US Navy enlisted rank, Petty Officer Second Class, E-5

PO3, US Navy enlisted rank, Petty Officer Third Class, E-4

PPI Display, traditional radar display equipment

RAV, Restricted Availability, short shipyard stay to make necessary repairs and routine maintenance of a ship

RIO, Radar Intercept Operator, the backseat guy in an F4 Phantom

RTC, Recruit Training Command, better known as 'boot camp'

RVN, Republic of Vietnam

Shore Patrol, (SP), Navy Military Police, (MP) Army Military Police

SOP, Standard Operating Procedure

SSQ-29, AN/SSQ-29, Original data terminal set for NTDS Link-11 data communication

TAD, naval term, 'Temporary Additional Duty', being transferred temporarily to another duty station

Trap, or Trap Onboard, the process of recovering (landing) on an aircraft carrier

UDT/SEAL, Underwater Demolition Team, SEAL team members are usually selected from UDT

USQ-36, AN/USQ-36, Newer style data terminal set for NTDS Link-11 data communication

Vultures Row, a balcony on the island structure of an aircraft carrier where crew members can safely observe flight operations

Yard Period, When the ship is in the shipyard for major repairs or overhaul

Wave, Female sailor

White Hat, the traditional enlisted sailor hat, also may refer to an enlisted sailor

WO-1, Warrant Officer, Warrant Officer Ranks are W-1 through W-5, specialist officer between enlisted and commissioned officer ranks

The USS *Ranger* DS Gang

Official Photo 22 February 1970, USS *Ranger* DS gang
DS-1 Newhard was promoted to Chief Petty Officer and was being transferred
I was also promoted to DS-1 right about this time

First Row – DS2 Lynn Smith, DS3 Chris Maschauer, DSC Dan Newhard, DS2 Gary Vanderbush, DS3 Tom Megow

Second Row – DS2 Dan Thompson, DS1 Ed Buselt, DS2 Duke Duquette (my number two man in data com), DS3 Setve Jochem, DS3 J. R. Williams

Third Row – DS3 Dean jones, unidentified, DS3 Ron Hammers (standing)

Forth Row – DS3 Jones, unidentified, DS2 Dick Svenson (Sven), DS3 Lyle Dreyer

ABOUT THE AUTHOR

Lynn B. Smith enlisted in the US Navy September 16, 1965 at age 17 and worked his way up from seaman apprentice to first class petty officer in less than five years. After attending electronics technician school and data system technician schools he was assigned to USS *Ranger* CVA-61 serving more than three years in *Ranger* before transfer to a final assignment in Virginia Beach Virginia.

In late 1971 he left the navy after six years active duty and started a career in electronics as a field service technician at Digital Equipment Corporation in the International Product Support Group in Maynard Massachusetts. In 1975 he moved to the 'Silicon Valley', San Jose California area, starting a 45-year career as an electronics design engineer, ending as Director of Hardware Engineering at Stem Inc. in December 2018.

Mr. Smith currently resides in Enterprise Alabama and remains active as an independent contractor in the energy storage and power electronics field and avionics instructor at the Alabama Aviation College in Ozark Alabama.